FREQUENCY
OF
EXCELLENCE

FREQUENCY

OF

EXCELLENCE

Tuning In to the Everyday Lessons
of Life and Leadership

SCOTT MILLSON

FREQUENCY OF EXCELLENCE
Tuning In to the Everyday Lessons of Life and Leadership

Copyright © 2024 by Scott Millson

Interior Layout and Design by Stephanie Anderson
Book Cover Design by Ron Boucher

ISBNs:
979-8-89165-164-7 *Paperback*
979-8-89165-165-4 *Hardback*
979-8-89165-166-1 *E-book*

Published by:
Streamline Books
Kansas City, MO
streamlinebookspublishing.com

*To my late father, my forever mentor, and to my
loving and supportive family—love y'all.*

*And to the women and men whose lessons and stories
grace these pages, thank you for your mentorship,
leadership, and, most importantly, friendship.*

*I am grateful to you all for allowing me to tune
in to your frequency of excellence.*

CONTENTS

SECTION 3: Management

SECTION 4: Sales

SECTION 5: Leadership

SECTION 6: Entrepreneurship

SECTION 7: Career Advice

INTRODUCTION

GROWING UP IN a small North Florida town, my roots are unmistakable and evident in three distinct traits: an unapologetic addiction to sweet tea, an overabundant use of the word "y'all," and my downright obsession with barbecue. I have long considered myself a sweet tea snob, but not just any sweet tea—it must be freshly brewed, and the sugar must be dissolved while the tea is warm. Adding sugar or, worse, artificial sweetener to previously made unsweet tea does not pass muster with me. As for my penchant for using the Southern conjunction for "you all," I have been unabashed in leveraging this highly efficient and linguistic masterpiece, even while living in New Jersey, where people would have preferred I use their quasi-conjunction "youz guyz." However, it is my affinity for BBQ that runs the deepest, and I have been known to chase the scent of hickory, cherry, or apple wood smoke for miles just to get a taste of that heavenly, wood-fired flavor.

My first taste of BBQ came in the mid-1970s when Sonny's BBQ opened their doors on Kingsley Avenue in Orange Park, Florida. My family would frequent this location often, and I have fond memories of caravaning to Sonny's with my Little League teammates following a big win at the ballfields. The parents would sit at one table, and eight dirty and grimy baseball players would cram into a booth made for four. My father loved Sonny's sweet-and-tangy baked beans, and I was a sucker for their hickory-smoked sliced pork. Although I have graduated to enjoying a broader array of BBQ goodness, I know from where my initial love of BBQ emanates.

This love of smoked meats only intensified later in my life as I became friends with a gentleman named John Rivers. Living in the same community in Central Florida, John and I became fast friends through mutual acquaintances; however, our friendship became stronger as we participated in a small men's group and discovered many common passions, including a mutual love of BBQ. To be clear, I love to eat BBQ, but John was exceptional at crafting it. John was so committed to this craft that in 2009, he left his executive position at a national pharmaceutical company to launch his own BBQ venture—4 Rivers Smokehouse. Since that time, 4 Rivers has dominated the Florida market and serves up the most delicious BBQ you'll ever taste. (It should also be noted that their sweet tea is extraordinary.)

As I had the opportunity to work with John and his team in initially expanding 4 Rivers, I came to appreciate his leadership style and business acumen. Over time, I was fortunate to call John a mentor as well as a friend. I learned a great deal from John and borrowed and adjusted many of his leadership philosophies, several of which are shared in the pages that follow.

One lesson I initially learned from John, and have since adapted, stands above the rest. It has become a cornerstone of my professional career and the foundation of this book. This lesson encourages us to pay attention and learn from the excellence that surrounds us in our everyday lives. John used a radio dial as a metaphor for how we achieve this growth, both as individuals and professionals.

As you read this book, you will be immersed in a deluge of radio waves as well as other oscillations on the electromagnetic spectrum. These invisible waves of sound and data are continuously flying in all directions around and through you, traveling at the speed of light. In order to slow down, capture, and process these imperceptible waves, you need a tuner of some sort. Even more importantly, the tuner must be dialed in to the exact right frequency to decode these packets of data and sound. If you aren't tuned in to the right frequency, you will only receive an annoying crackle of static, and any perceptible sounds would not be memorable.

The same is true for both our professional and personal lives. At any given moment of any given day, there are lessons to be learned all around us. As humans, we are able to receive and decipher the sound and data waves that surround us, but we are often so distracted that we miss the opportunity to truly *experience* them. When we aren't paying close attention—aren't tuned in—these lessons are full of static or simply missed altogether. When this happens, opportunities for growth pass us by at the speed of light, gone forever. However, when we *are* tuned in to the right frequency, we recognize the examples of excellence occurring around us, and we store those memories for reflection downstream.

We live in a world where multitasking is celebrated, and we intentionally overload our senses, searching for that next dopamine hit. Our attention spans are shorter than they ever have been, and our focus has never been so easily diverted. "Look, squirrel" has become an unfortunate and too common meme in today's society, mocking our collective inability to slow down and absorb the rich lessons that surround us.

Much like harnessing a radio wave, we must adjust the dial on our own tuners, identify the right frequency, and absorb the lessons that would otherwise pass us by. Our ability to grow and develop as people and professionals relies on our ability to find our *frequency of excellence* as well as the frequencies of those around us.

My professional career has been characterized by excellence, not necessarily by anything I was able to accomplish, but because of the company I kept and organizations with which I was fortunate to be associated. Many of the leaders with whom I've worked are considered among the very best at their craft—leading billion-dollar organizations to unparalleled levels of success. Yet my influences didn't stop with just leadership excellence. I worked for and alongside some of the industry's greatest consultants, salespeople, managers, communicators, entrepreneurs, strategic thinkers, operational wizards, and problem solvers—people who made excellence an everyday occurrence.

Two gifts stand out as important in my career: (1) I had a front-row seat to witness excellence in action across several industries, organizations, and leadership styles; and (2) I was gifted with keen observational skills that allowed me to consistently find the frequency of excellence and store those lessons for downstream reflection. In leveraging these two gifts, I was able to piece together a successful career that spanned across multiple decades, including time spent in rigid, chain-of-command organizations, as well as multi-billion-dollar matrixed organizations. This book intends to shine a light on the lessons I've learned during my career and on the people who so gracefully demonstrated that excellence.

In building upon these two gifts, I developed a unique style of leading that I call *reflective leadership.* Reflective leadership is the ability of a leader to successfully tune in to and harness past experiences, networks, relationships, successes, and even failures to inspire and motivate themselves and their teams to achieve success. The experiences of a reflective leader come in various forms, shapes, and sizes. The reflection can be as dramatic and obvious as witnessing a mentor lead a team through a challenging situation, or it can be as subtle as being inspired by your daughter and how she handles her own challenging health situation. Regardless of the origin, the reflective leader, when tuned in to the right frequency, can successfully recall past situations to guide them or their teams through a difficult time or toward a desired outcome.

A successful and resourceful reflective leader is made up of thousands of life experiences diligently pooled together in a collection of these reflections, or what I refer to as a *Reflection Collection.* These stored experiences and reflections are then tapped into when the situation requires a leader to act, react, or lead.

Any modicum of success I've been able to achieve has come directly from these experiences and leveraging my Reflection Collection. My own Collection is made up of the memories of and experiences with the mentors that shaped me, many of which are shared within this book. I've called regularly on these experiences, and they have guided me throughout my career.

The art of management, sales, entrepreneurship, and leadership lies in simple, everyday common sense actions and activities. The key is to pay attention, identify, and reflect upon the profound impact of these simplicities. For reasons that will be explored later, I was blessed with an ability to slow down, spot excellence, observe, and apply these lessons to my life and profession. Quite simply, I tuned in to the frequency of excellence as it surrounded me and added those lessons to my Collection.

I believe many of today's business-oriented books can be overly academic, conceptual, and esoteric. I am none of these things. I am an everyman and darn proud of it. I do not own an advanced degree and didn't attend an Ivy League school. I come from very humble beginnings and have worked my tail off to achieve any small sliver of success. This book is not chock-full of academic research, nor is it sharing any new groundbreaking leadership principles. It is my attempt to share with others the excellence that I found hidden in plain sight throughout my career and the wisdom I gleaned through those experiences. As such, the lessons and stories I share are meant to be encouraging and suggestive.

I have always believed lessons are most easily learned when shared as stories, as storytelling has forever been one of our most powerful means of communication. Storytelling is powerful because of its ability to engage, inspire, and connect with an audience on an emotional and intellectual level. The stories that are shared within this book are intended to achieve those very objectives and move you both emotionally and intellectually.

This book serves as a valuable professional resource to use throughout your career. Several of the chapters offer quick, yet impactful lessons, while others delve deeper into their subjects. Regardless of length, you can find a topic that is of interest or relevant to your current situation, read it, digest it, and then revisit as needed. Each lesson stands on its own, yet they are all intertwined by the way in which they were learned and the stories which bind them together.

In the first section of this book, I provide a brief overview of my life and career. This book is not a memoir; however, understanding my path from enlistment in the US Navy to becoming one of the youngest partners in a multi-billion-dollar, global consulting firm provides context for the reflective lessons and stories I share.

Each of the lessons on the pages that follow are etched into my mind and hold a special place in my heart; however, they are my memories, and any inaccuracies are mine and mine alone. When appropriate and with permissions granted, I have used the names of the colleagues and mentors who have graciously shared their experiences with me. Whether openly named or not, these friends, colleagues, and mentors provided me with invaluable lessons that I would now like to share with you.

Whether you are new to the workforce or an established professional, work for a small company or a multi-billion-dollar global organization, we all have the ability to observe, listen, and learn—to find our unique frequency. The degree to which you consciously decide to *truly* observe and store the observation for downstream reflection and utilization can set you apart from others. Be on the lookout for the potential lessons that surround you, even when you believe excellence is nowhere in sight—because we can and should learn through both success and failure.

Finally, my hope is that you are encouraged as you read this book—encouraged to learn from the lessons that shaped me and encouraged to move forward, observe, and build your own Reflection Collection. Even better, my ultimate hope is you, personally, become part of someone else's Collection in the years that follow. Serving as a coach or mentor for someone else and watching their career flourish is a joy akin to watching a child grow into the man or woman they were meant to be. There is no greater joy than knowing you helped someone else be great.

The secret to your success lies in your ability to slow down and observe the excellence that surrounds you, store those lessons in your own Reflection Collection, and then call upon those lessons when the time is right.

Find your frequency of excellence and be great!

My Story, My Path

CHAPTER 1

Don't Miss the Gorilla (or the Banana)

The only thing worse than being blind
is having sight but no vision.
—HELEN KELLER

O NE OF MY favorite high school teachers was a man named Dr. Bill Nulty. Not only was Dr. Nulty a great teacher of history, but also as a former soccer coach and retired Marine Corps lieutenant colonel, we found several common interests over which we could bond. He knew my family well and wouldn't hesitate to call on me in class or put me on the spot. He was exceptional at engaging his students and always found creative ways to introduce historical topics. As a result, I wasn't overly surprised when he pulled me aside before a morning class to ask if I could help him with that day's subject on eyewitness accounts and how unreliable they can often be.

Dr. Nulty informed me he was going to open the day by making some form of a statement, and he wanted me to immediately take the other side of the argument. He often encouraged discord as it related to topical conversations, so I figured this was going to be one of those typical and engaging Dr. Nulty lessons; however, as he proceeded, it quickly became clear this lesson would be anything but typical. He instructed me to be very strong with my opinion, and he would, in turn, counter with equally direct responses. He encouraged

3

me to take it to a ten on a scale of one to ten. His only request was that we not use profane language or take any personal shots at one another, but he wanted the argument to be heated and loud—the louder, the better. We were to engage in this heated discourse for about five minutes, at which point he was going to announce I was being sent to the dean's office for severe insubordination.

Now, unbeknownst to me, he had also pulled another student aside and asked them to participate in this unique lesson. The other student was to remain in their seat for the first two to three minutes, and then she was to rise from her seat, walk to the front of the room, open a cabinet, take out a banana, eat it, and return to her seat—all while Dr. Nulty and I were yelling at one another.

I loved where this was going and gave what I thought was an Oscar-worthy performance. The fabricated argument went well, everyone's eyes were fixated on me, and their jaws appropriately had dropped to the floor.

Once Dr. Nulty announced I was being sent to the dean's office and I left the room in an animated huff, he asked everyone to take out a sheet of paper and write down *exactly* what had just occurred in the classroom. He encouraged everyone to write every single detail on their sheets of paper so the dean could fully understand what just happened.

After he gathered the sheets of paper, he called for me to return from the hallway. He then shared with the class that I was actually not in trouble but had been asked to participate in a fabricated dispute as part of the day's lesson. When he communicated that the student eating the banana was also part of the lesson, the room fell eerily quiet as the vast majority of the class had no idea what he was talking about. They'd never seen the student get up to eat the banana.

Dr. Nulty's primary point of the lesson was that we, as humans, often fail to perceive something because our attention is focused elsewhere—we are often terrible eyewitnesses and miss things that are hidden in plain sight. For obvious reasons, this lesson stuck with me over the years and served as a constant reminder for me to have my eyes open at all times and be observant of all that is around me.

Although the term was not coined until several years after my high school graduation, the concept Dr. Nulty was trying to introduce was something called *inattentional blindness.*[1] The term *inattentional blindness* was initially created by psychologists Arien Mack, PhD, and Irvin Rock, PhD, but became more well known when two Harvard University psychologists (Christopher Chabris, PhD, and Daniel Simons, PhD) conducted an experiment that would have made Dr. Nulty proud.[2] In the experiment, the researchers asked participants to watch a video of six people, three of whom were wearing white T-shirts and three of whom were wearing black T-shirts, tossing a basketball back and forth, while moving about a room.

The observers in the research study were instructed to count the number of times the people wearing white shirts passed the ball to one another. Counting the number of basketball passes required significant focus because of the constant movement on the screen and the fact that the ball was continually being passed, both high and low. Unbeknownst to the observers in the study, a woman dressed in a gorilla suit was instructed to walk through the middle of the six people, thump her chest, and then exit the screen. At the end of the video, the observers were asked to share the number of passes made by the white-shirted team. Once the answer was provided, they were also asked if they had noticed anything unusual. Nearly 50 percent of all participants entirely missed the gorilla. Their inattentional blindness essentially made the gorilla invisible!

We are all victims of inattentional blindness. It can strike at any time of any day and we miss our version of the gorilla. Sometimes the gorilla is a coworker struggling with a task, and you miss the opportunity to offer a helping hand. Other times you may miss an example a leader sets because you're too focused on achieving a specific outcome, or you miss the opportunity to learn from a gifted coworker in a sales meeting because you're obsessing over your portion of the pitch. In all these situations, we miss the proverbial gorilla and the literal opportunity to learn, grow, and develop. We aren't tuned to the right frequency.

In today's world, inattentional blindness is a growing epidemic. The world has taken multitasking to unprecedented levels and we are rewarding people because of their ability to keep twenty balls in the air at the same time. Instead, we should be encouraging people to focus on fewer things and learn more from those situations. Whether it is our mobile devices, social media, or a constant stream of video, beeps, and buzzes, our attention is divided unlike any other time in history.

Luckily for me and for whatever the reason, I was able to remain focused during the stories that are captured within the chapters of this book. In each of these situations, there were a host of things that could have diverted my attention from the lessons being taught. Instead, I was able to observe, listen, and learn.

I stated above I am not sure why I have been able to remain focused during the experiences that are the basis of this book. That isn't entirely accurate, although my "why" is more of a feeling and lacks any clinical diagnoses. For my entire life, I have been accused of being unable to sit still, needing to be in constant movement (my foot is tapping a mile a minute as I write this), being impulsive and forgetful, and being hyperfocused on the task at hand. These traits have never negatively affected me, my behavior, or my work performance, but they are who I am. Given that I am a parent to a now-adult child who shares similar traits and actually was diagnosed with attention deficit and hyperactivity disorder at an early age, I have become keenly aware of this superpower. I believe my ability to witness the excellence you'll read about in these pages was bolstered by my ability to block out some of the daily noise to tune in and experience and learn from the lessons being shared with me.

Please note I intentionally chose to use the word *superpower* above because I truly believe it leans significantly more toward a superpower than it does a disorder. There is a host of books that address this topic, and this isn't one of them, but I did want to call attention to anyone who may have this diagnosed or undiagnosed superpower, in that inattentional blindness may not be as applicable to you, and you can use that to your advantage to focus, observe, and store the lessons that surround you.

Max Planck, quantum theorist and Nobel Prize winner, once wrote, "When you change the way you look at things, the things you look at change." My encouragement for you is to slow down, change how you look at everyday things, absorb the lessons, and piece them into your Reflection Collection.

Be on the lookout for your gorillas (and bananas).

CHAPTER 2

My Blueprint

I consider myself the
luckiest man on the face of the earth.
—LOU GEHRIG

I MUST HAVE WATCHED the movie *Pride of the Yankees*, a 1942
movie starring Gary Cooper, dozens of times as a child. Why a
Southern boy who was only casually interested in baseball and
grew up in the 1970s would want to watch a black-and-white movie
about Lou Gehrig, the legendary New York Yankees baseball player
who would die at an early age of a horrible disease that now bears
his name, is beyond me. At face value, I should have quickly skipped
past that movie on the television and sought out something in color
or with considerably more action. But I didn't. I was drawn to the
story, the characters, and maybe even the black-and-white nature
of the film. For whatever the reason, Lou Gehrig quickly became a
hero of mine, and I sought out any information I could find on his
life and what made him the Iron Horse of baseball.

Given the movie is over eighty years old at the time of this book
being published, I think it is a fair to assume the vast majority of
you have not seen *Pride of the Yankees*, so allow me to summarize
it in under a hundred words: Lou Gehrig was a first-generation
American, son of German immigrants, living in New York City in the
1920s. Lou was of average intelligence, although his baseball skills
allowed him to attend Columbia University. He ultimately signed

with the New York Yankees and played alongside Babe Ruth. When he finally got his turn and was moved into the starting lineup, he played 2,130 consecutive games, a then-MLB record. He was known for his hard work, modesty, perseverance, and his farewell speech in Yankee Stadium in which he declares himself the "luckiest man on the face of the earth."

Although I was unaware at the time, the hours I spent watching *Pride of the Yankees* were exceptionally formative and set me on a path for my life and my career—striving to live like the Iron Horse. I recall being proud in elementary school when I received a perfect attendance award, never missing a day of school—just like Lou. This carried forward into my junior and senior high school years, fighting through illnesses and wearing my perfect attendance as a badge of honor.

I also seemed to align myself with Lou in terms of how hard he had to work to keep up with others. In terms of athletics and academics, I often felt I had to outwork others to achieve or maintain top performance. Athletically, I was always decent at the sport of my choice, but if I wanted to be above average, I would have to put in a great deal of work and shed pounds of sweat. By junior high, it was pretty evident my skinny frame was best suited for running longer distances, and so track and field/cross country became my sport of choice. I was an all-area runner and four-year varsity athlete in high school, but if I had not logged the thousands of miles that were necessary to succeed, I would have gravitated to just above the mean. I had to put in the work, just like Lou.

When it came to academics, once again, I had to outwork others to achieve my goals. I was born with great parents and good genes, as both my mother and father were highly intelligent and educated, but I had to put forth significant effort to achieve good grades. However, even with those genes and the significant hours I invested in studying, I never in my entire academic career achieved straight As. Never. I remember being close in the ninth grade, but I received a B+ in algebra, and Mrs. Fisher refused to bump me to an A, even though I tried and argued every angle. (I don't blame her, by the way, as I didn't earn the A.) I also did not perform well on standardized tests and scored just barely high enough to be accepted into the University of Florida (UF). Once at UF, I had to work harder than my peers to achieve good grades. I would spend hours in the campus library studying while watching many of my friends treat their library visit as a social hour. That was not my path. I couldn't afford social hours, as I needed to apply those same hours to studying. I had to work extra hard to graduate with a solid GPA and to land a good first job with a great employer.

My first "real job" was with the United States Navy and the Naval Reserves. As I entered college in 1985, I had an agreement with my parents—they would pay for half of my schooling, and I would pay the other half. My parents' (appropriate and accurate) rationale was I would take college more seriously and would be more engaged if it was my own money being invested in my future. In an effort to build an adequate college fund, I worked my tail off during high school years, balancing varsity sports and a rigorous work schedule while also taking honors/college-prep courses.

Over the summers, I would grind to make as much money as possible, acting like a squirrel trying to gather as many nuts as possible to get me through the winter months. There were two summers when my squirrel (and Lou Gehrig–like) tendencies were on full display. For the summer of 1985, I worked two jobs that would have me pulling sixteen-hour daily shifts. I flipped hamburgers at McDonald's from 7:00 a.m. to 3:00 p.m., then went home, showered, and changed into my Steak & Ale uniform to work an evening shift from 4:00 p.m. to midnight as a busboy. After a relatively good night's sleep, I would wake up and begin the lather-rinse-repeat cycle to gather more nuts. The other summer job that stands out was a graveyard shift (7:00 p.m. to 7:00 a.m.) at a canning plant where I worked an assembly line watching Budweiser lids get stamped and formed from a giant roll of aluminum.

These summer jobs were not the most glamorous, but they fulfilled a role and were helpful in teaching me the value of hard work and doing whatever it took to achieve an objective. Even with those efforts and my frugal nature, I found myself short of my savings goals and came to the realization midway through my freshman year at Florida that, if nothing changed, I would be unable to make it through college without accumulating student debt.

It was during this time of struggle my mother received a fateful call from a naval recruiter, and he threw me a lifeline. His offer was for me to join a new naval program called SAM (Sea/Air Mariner), which was designed to recruit college students to join the Navy to augment our country's Naval Reserves. The program would have me attend boot camp over the summer, return to college in the fall, and immediately begin service in the Reserves. Although I was intrigued by the offer, my mother was mortified as she came from three generations of US Naval Academy graduates and naval officers and wasn't initially keen on the idea of me joining the Navy as an enlisted man. That said, she understood my financial predicament and stepped aside to allow me to make my own decision and forge my own path.

My enlistment in the spring of 1986 was one of the best decisions of my life. The experiences I gained that summer in boot camp, along with the monthly repetition of attending my naval drill weekends, provided me with incredible opportunities for growth and development. I understood my collegiate experience would be different than 99 percent of other UF students, but I was more than happy to forgo one weekend a month of partying so I could complete college without debt and have the opportunity to jumpstart my professional career.

My enlistment in the Navy made my experience at UF harder than most, but hard work was nothing new.

Just like Lou.

CHAPTER 3

My Foundation: Hewitt Associates
1990–2006

> You can't build a great building on a weak foundation.
> You must have a solid foundation if you're
> going to have a strong superstructure.
> —GORDON B. HINCKLEY

I N THE BACK half of my senior year at UF, I received quite possibly one of the greatest blessings of my life when I received an offer to join Hewitt Associates, a global HR/benefits consulting firm based in Chicago, Illinois. Hewitt was one of the most sought-after companies that came onto college campuses in the late 1980s, and I was happy to have received an invitation to interview. Hewitt was extraordinarily well respected in the consulting world and had a stellar reputation as being a special place to work. So much so, Hewitt was formally recognized as one of the "100 Best Companies to Work for in America" in a book published in the late 1980s. My offer was to join Hewitt in the Atlanta office, and I enthusiastically jumped at the opportunity.

As you'll read in the chapters that follow, any sliver of professional success I've been able to achieve came from my initial seventeen years with Hewitt. It is the foundation of who I am today as a leader, manager, consultant, salesperson, and communicator. As most anyone who worked at or with Hewitt pre-2000s would agree it was a special environment. From the leadership to the quality of work and client relationships, Hewitt offered a daily master class in excellence.

You've probably heard the adage "a high tide lifts all boats." Hewitt was the tide that lifted all our boats. From the people they hired to the high-quality standards the organization required, we, most notably me, were all buoyed by the brilliance that was Hewitt Associates.

The frequency of excellence at Hewitt emitted a powerful signal—excellence was everywhere, and it was captivating.

When I joined privately held Hewitt Associates in January 1990, we were a few thousand associates strong, with a few hundred partners. The culture of Hewitt was unique. Some of the aspects that attracted me from the jump included uniform office sizes, business cards without titles, free breakfast and lunches for all, and a uniquely flat and matrixed organizational structure. All these attributes and more created an egoless environment in which everyone was focused on serving our clients exceptionally well and consistently delivering quality services. To achieve these external goals, Hewitt set one of their three primary tenants with an inward focus—to "create a SWE" (satisfying work experience) for all associates. Given Hewitt's partnership structure, we were encouraged to stretch ourselves to grab at the brass ring of partnership through hard work, exceptional client service, and billable hours.

From day one at Hewitt, I was intensely focused on becoming a Hewitt partner. My personal goal was to be invited into the partnership by the end of my tenth year with the firm, and I would work as hard as necessary to achieve this goal. From every client I served to every project I assumed, I performed to the best of my ability. I volunteered for the tough assignments. I worked long hours. I poured everything I had into Hewitt, and it was noticed. In the fall of 1999, just three months before my tenth anniversary and just following my thirty-second birthday, I seized the brass ring and was invited to become one of the youngest partners at Hewitt.

At my first partner meeting in the fall of 1999, the primary agenda item was for the partners to evaluate a new e-business that Hewitt was considering to capitalize on the massive growth in internet adoption and the rapid growth of valuations for new dot-com start-ups. It was a wildly interesting social and economic time in the United States, and Hewitt was looking to take advantage of the opportunity by being the first to market with a unique, internet-based healthcare product.

Just prior to the partner meeting, the leader of my then-current business unit (president, ostensibly), Tom Schmitz, asked to have a few moments with me. He gave me a preview of the e-business to be discussed at the following day's meeting. At the end of the preview, he asked me to join him in launching this new business for Hewitt. My reaction was an equal mix of being stunned, shocked, and excited. As I sat through the following day's presentation, my excitement overtook the other two emotions, and I was ready to dive headfirst into this new business, which would ultimately be called Sageo. I pushed all my chips into the middle of the table and joined Tom and a few other partners in leading the Sageo business.

Working alongside the other Sageo leaders was one of, if not the, most influential times in my career. My learning curve was as steep as it had ever been. I was being exposed to business leaders I had only previously admired from afar and was slowly adding them to a growing list of mentors, most notably Sageo's CEO, Tom Schmitz. Tom was an industry pioneer and was a key component of Hewitt's rich history and culture. My decision to join the Sageo business provided me with a front-row seat to excellence, watching, listening, and learning from leaders like Tom.

My career trajectory had changed forever, and nearly all of it was for the positive. However, as we got further into the year, there was one not-so-minor detail beginning to raise its head—Hewitt's intention to spin Sageo off as its own entity meant I was going to have to resign my newly acquired partnership at Hewitt.

Gulp.

The Hewitt partner title that I had worked so hard to obtain was politely being pulled from my grasp and through my own doing. Toward the end of the year, I was formally presented with a choice to step back from Sageo and rejoin Hewitt with my partnership status intact or resign the partnership and continue with Sageo as a founding member. It could and should have been one of the more difficult decisions in my career, but it really wasn't. I was all in with Sageo.

I have never worked as hard as I did in late 1999 and 2000, and yet I've also never had as much fun or grown as much during those same years. I was spending weeks upon weeks in San Francisco and Chicago, working tirelessly with our team and partners building out the Sageo.com business, website, insurance carrier relationships, processes, and call center. Simon Sinek famously wrote, "Working hard for something we don't care about is called stress. Working hard for something we love is called passion." I was extremely passionate about Sageo and the work we were doing. Eighty-to-ninety-hour workweeks weren't stressful—they were enjoyable because I loved the people with whom I was working and the incredible business we were building. We were blazing new trails in healthcare and the market was reacting favorably. My frequency was locked in on Sageo, and I was learning at a dizzying rate.

It was a time unlike any other in my career, right up until the dot-com bubble began to deflate—quickly.

In addition to the broader US economic challenges of the dot-com bubble, we ran into two primary challenges with Sageo: (1) the product was ahead of its time by nearly ten years, as evidenced by a host of similarly designed and successful companies launching in 2010 and beyond, and (2) Hewitt partners were appropriately questioning whether Sageo's return on investment would be stronger within the walls of Hewitt versus running it as a separate entity.

So, after two years with Sageo being run as its own company, with its own set of executives, website, and salesforce, we were folded back into Hewitt Associates to gain economies of scale. As a result, our business model and market focus were also tweaked. It was a necessary transition, but it wasn't easy. In Hewitt's attempt to quickly capitalize on the dot-com era by running Sageo as a separate entity and building unique and independent websites and processes, we burned through a lot of capital, which obviously presented a real challenge for the partnership.

Thankfully, the majority of former Sageo executives who had just a year prior resigned our partnership, were allowed to rejoin Hewitt. Our partnership positions were reinstated and our historical capital accounts restored, but it was an appropriately bumpy reentry. Unfortunately, not all roles were reintegrated. Tom's role as Sageo's CEO, for example, was eliminated for obvious reasons as were several other duplicative leadership positions. It was, however, a testament to the strength of Hewitt's unparalleled and supportive culture that allowed for the majority of us to be successfully reintegrated.

Although Sageo didn't achieve the original goals the partners had set forth, it serves as one of the greatest lessons of my career and one that I reflect upon constantly. It also personified the Wayne Gretsky quote for me, in that "you miss 100 percent of the shots you don't take." My fellow Hewitt partners and I felt Sageo was a shot worth taking in 1999, and we took it. We swung hard but missed, some of it by our doing and some of it by encountering the broader US economic challenges.

The business didn't turn out as we had hoped, but a great deal of good did come from Sageo. Upon reintegration, Sageo was transformed into what was called Health and Welfare Enterprise and served as the foundation of Hewitt's foray into a new market—the middle market. I'm quite proud of the fact that the middle market business unit still exists today, nearly twenty-five years later—serving hundreds of clients and employing hundreds of employees. I was fortunate to be asked to lead the business upon reintegration in 2001, and I proudly led our teams through that difficult period, learning and growing through those unique experiences.

After leading the former Sageo business for several years, I was asked to lead another new business venture for Hewitt called Your Spending Account (YSA). Hewitt had long been asked by our client councils to perform this service and in 2003, we ultimately pulled the trigger. As with any new business venture, it came with considerable growth opportunities and unique experiences—along with a few bumps and bruises. We built new technologies and were at the forefront of implementing new processes and leveraging our global capabilities with our team in India. YSA provided me with unique opportunities and created a host of experiences upon which I've reflected often over the last twenty years. Some of these experiences were successes, and many were failures, but all were great learning opportunities that helped further shape me as a leader, and I am happy to share many of those learnings with you in the pages that follow.

From a broader firm perspective, after a great deal of discussion and consideration of the partners, Hewitt Associates became a public entity on June 27, 2002. Firm leadership and the majority of partners felt this was a necessary step in our evolution, and at the time, it seemed like an appropriate step to take. In the preceding sixty years, Hewitt had achieved unparalleled success as a private organization, and we had established ourselves as the gold standard in the HR and benefits consulting industry.

Although I was clearly biased, I believe Hewitt was at the very top of the food chain and was constantly looked upon to set and drive the market. However, the industry was also going through a metamorphosis of sorts, and the size, volume, and scope of HR and benefit outsourcing contracts required a level of capital investments a privately held organization would struggle to support. Additionally, it was becoming clear that Hewitt's desire to strategically acquire industry assets and grow revenue would benefit greatly from having our own publicly traded stock to use as currency.

While I believe the decision to IPO was, in fact, the right one made at the right time, I also believe it was one part of the reason Hewitt began to lose its grip on the pole position in our industry. Slowly but surely, the uniqueness of Hewitt's culture began to change, and for the first time in my career, I started to question whether I would retire at Hewitt. Over the years following the IPO, this was a common yet unfortunate growing and uneasy sentiment running through the former partnership group and beyond.

This sentiment was so strong and so widely held that an unfortunate and associated moniker was soon attached to it—Flight 627. There was a growing belief that many former partners would be departing the organization on June 27, 2006, four years removed from IPO date and the same date former partner shares would become fully vested. For reasons that spilled beyond the IPO, Hewitt did experience a good bit of senior turnover in the latter half of 2006, including me. After an amazing ride of nearly seventeen years and a memory bank that overflowed, I resigned from Hewitt Associates to explore new opportunities and obtain new experiences.

I wouldn't have traded one minute of those seventeen years. I personally and professionally benefited greatly from the high tide that was known as Hewitt Associates. The leaders, consultants, sales professionals, and managers I had the pleasure of working for and alongside were beyond exceptional and without peer in our industry.

That said, it was time for me to move on, further grow and develop, and share with others the excellence I had observed and experienced at Hewitt.

It was time for me to change my frequency.

CHAPTER 4

My Bridge: CoAdvantage/PlanSource

2006–2010

The first step towards getting somewhere is to decide
that you are not going to stay where you are.

—J. P. MORGAN

U PON MY ARRIVAL at CoAdvantage, an Orlando-based HR outsourcing (HRO) and professional employer organization firm, I felt like a fish out of water. I was stepping into an established organization without any real or existing relationships within the company. Like Toto and Dorothy, I was clearly not in Kansas anymore. Furthering my fish/water feeling was the fact that many people on the CoAdvantage team had been working together for nearly ten years, since the organization's inception. This experience was new to me in that I'd not been on a "first date" in seventeen years. At Hewitt, even with relocating two times, I had an institutional reputation, and I was able to positively utilize this throughout my time at Hewitt. At CoAdvantage, I did not have this advantage, and I spent my four years there working to build relationships from the ground up and not being able to readily rely on things I'd done in my past. It turned out to be a great experience for me and provided many opportunities for reflection and growth.

Hewitt was a global organization, with a plethora of Fortune 500 companies as our clients. CoAdvantage was a regional company, with deep roots within the Orlando small-business community and an entrepreneurial culture that was palpable. While I was excited about the transition from Hewitt to CoAdvantage, the lessons I learned and the experiences I gained were even greater than anticipated. Most specifically, I learned how to operate within and with small businesses, and our clients reminded me daily that client service is client service, regardless of the size of the organization.

I was initially hired into the chief operating officer role at CoAdvantage—overseeing all three of our business units. Two of these three businesses were new to me, and I found myself staring up a very steep learning curve but loving the opportunity to learn new things and stretch myself. Within a year, we reorganized the business and I moved into the role of president of CoAdvantage's HRO business, which was more aligned with my experiences at Hewitt. We also took the opportunity to acquire an emerging technology company called PlanSource, which ultimately became the key driver of CoAdvantage's (and successor company's) business. It was my first real experience of being near the driver's seat of an acquisition and subsequent integration, and it provided me with an opportunity to, once again, learn and grow.

At the end of the day, my four years at CoAdvantage gave me a slew of great experiences and encouragement, but there were two that stand out to me and provided me with opportunities for downstream reflections: (1) the desire and opportunity to give back to our communities; and (2) an entrepreneurial itch that needed to be scratched. For the former, CoAdvantage was well known in our community as being a selfless organization that freely gave back to the community that gave them their start. I was encouraged from the get-go to be involved and to build relationships throughout Orlando. CoAdvantage helped shrink the world for me and had me thinking and acting more locally than globally. For the latter, the entrepreneurial spirit that was initially sparked by my father when he ran his own company from 1974 to 1992 was reignited by the entire team at CoAdvantage. I experienced the highs and lows of running a small business and how the smallest of decisions and economic events, both locally and globally, can affect an organization.

My time at CoAdvantage was critical to my development in so many ways and served as a necessary bridge of strength and confidence to help me successfully launch my own firm, which I did on July 1, 2010—the biggest leap of faith of my life.

CHAPTER 5

My Destination:
MillsonJames/HUB International
2010–2023

Success is not the key to happiness.
Happiness is the key to success. If you love what
you are doing, you will be successful.
—ALBERT SCHWEITZER

U PON GRADUATION FROM Harvard MBA School in 1963, my father, Warner Millson, set out on a career of corporate finance and audit with world-class organizations like Arthur Andersen. While he enjoyed his professional career, he loved two things even more: his family and his entrepreneurial spirit. It was with these two loves in mind that he chose family over corporate America and, in 1974, moved our family from the frigid temperatures of the Midwest to the sunny and humid skies of Florida. With three children under the age of ten, he purchased the assets of a retail store in Orange Park, Florida, and launched Millson Enterprises (d/b/a Arts & Crafts). My father built a great retail business and was doing well right up until Sam Walton and Walmart came to town in the late 1980s.

Walmart's arrival brought instantaneous challenges. My father couldn't compete with Walmart's pricing or diversity of products, particularly during recessionary times. I vividly recall watching one of the smartest and greatest businessmen I knew begin to question his career and business decisions. No one wants to see their childhood hero struggle, particularly an impressionable twenty-two-year-old college student.

In my last semester at UF, I took a course on strategic business planning in which we had to diagnose the challenges and opportunities of opening a retail convenience store in a small town. This exercise hit very close to home and uncovered some developing phobias that had been bubbling beneath the surface as I watched my father struggle to keep his once-thriving business afloat. As I worked to develop the summation of my semester-ending paper, it was difficult to set those emotions aside. As a result, my paper read as a cautionary tale—highlighting all the negatives of this convenience store business and the multitude of reasons why it should not be launched.

The paper was unnecessarily negative, as the scars of my father's situation and tail-end challenges of his entrepreneurial endeavor came rushing to the surface and found their ways into the written word of my paper. It was in those moments I vowed to never own my own business in an effort to avoid a similar fate.

The good news is life provides us with opportunities to grow and modify the statements we make or beliefs we hold earlier in life. We are not locked in by blood oaths—we are given daily opportunities to write and rewrite our stories. I'm sure when I wrote that paper in 1989, I was crystal clear on what I wanted and didn't want in life. Thankfully for me, I was given the opportunity to grow and experience new and different things in the years that followed. In those years, I was exposed to extraordinary leaders and entrepreneurs who helped ease the pain of those scars and presented me with new opportunities to see entrepreneurship in a new and more positive light.

There will always be challenges in life and in business. There is no debating this truism. However, as the saying goes, you cannot discover new oceans unless you have the courage to lose sight of the shore. My experience with Hewitt, Sageo, and CoAdvantage gave me the experience and courage to rewrite my story, lose sight of the shore, and launch my own consulting firm in 2010—MillsonJames.

I am 100 percent certain the twenty-two-year-old me would have shuddered at the idea of abandoning an executive position with a handsome salary, with a growing company, and with four children aged fourteen and younger. Then again, the younger me also would have balked at the idea of resigning his partnership with a global consulting firm months removed from receiving a life-fulfilling invitation. We are blessed with the ability to learn from our experiences but only if we are open to listening to and reflecting upon them.

Launching and running MillsonJames was one of the greatest and most rewarding experiences of my life. I was able to immediately and tangibly see the fruits of my labor. It was a daily bet I was placing on myself, and I was thrilled to watch the cards be played in my favor. Even when the cards didn't get dealt as I had hoped, I had no one to blame but myself and could quickly self-correct and take things in a different direction.

I came to realize and appreciate that I am my own best lottery ticket.

Given we had four young children at the time, which came with their own set of unique challenges and sometimes significant expenses, I should have experienced sleepless nights with unbelievable bouts of anxiety. I did not. From the initial launch, I had an unexplainable sense of peace. All my experiences pointed toward one thought: I was doing what I should be. It wasn't easy by any stretch of the imagination, but hard work had never been foreign to me, and I willingly embraced it.

The experiences I gained running MillsonJames were second only to the foundational experiences I had at Hewitt. The lessons were daily and came with great impact. I have stockpiled those memories and have used them every day since. A good number of the chapters that follow stem from what I learned leading up to launching MillsonJames as well as the entrepreneurial experiences I've gained since. More specifically, many of these lessons came as a result of specific actions I took when I made the decision to venture out on my own.

As you'll read in a future chapter, I was encouraged by a recommendation made by my father-in-law, Dr. H. Russell Fogler, to learn from and lean on others who had experienced something I wished to experience. So, in the months leading up to and through the launch of MillsonJames, I scheduled many meetings, coffees, and lunches with friends and colleagues who had launched their own firms. The goal of these meetings was to learn from them and understand their stories, the challenges they faced, and the opportunities they uncovered. In every single one of these meetings, I gleaned some new information that propelled me forward. I'm grateful for every one of these meetings—many of which are highlighted within this book.

We had an incredible run at MillsonJames, which continued through our acquisition by HUB International in 2017. If I'm being completely honest, I had zero intentions of ever selling my company. It wasn't anywhere on my radar or in any business plan I'd written. We had built an exceptional lifestyle company that afforded me the opportunity to call my own shots and choose when I wanted to hit the gas or tap the brakes. I didn't foresee a capital transaction in my future as I didn't believe what we had built was marketable to a potential suitor.

A few years earlier, in the late 2000s, I had considered buying a company that was somewhat similar to MillsonJames. However, the owner and I could never come to an agreement on structure or price because the business was wrapped up in one individual, the owner, and once he left, the revenues would likely leave with him. The owner had painted himself into a corner and, candidly, I was feeling the same in 2017 with MillsonJames. The difference was I was comfortable running MillsonJames as a lifestyle company without the potential of a capital transaction, that is, until a fateful lunch with a friend and former client opened my eyes to a new and different reality.

Upon launching MillsonJames in 2010, my initial sales calls were to friends and colleagues who were in the insurance industry. I called each of them to introduce MillsonJames and to paint a picture of the value I thought we could deliver together. One of those calls was to a former fraternity brother and longtime friend, Chris Gardner, who was a partner in a local firm named KuykendallGardner (KG). Chris was gracious to hire MillsonJames in 2010 and we had immediate and sustained success with KG, which lasted right up and initially through KG's acquisition by HUB International in 2014. A few months following the acquisition, Chris notified me they would no longer need MillsonJames' services, given HUB had similar resources of which they could now take advantage. I completely understood this rationale and thanked him for helping us get our start several years earlier.

As I fast-forward to 2017, I reached out to Chris, who was now CEO of HUB International Florida, to see if there was any opportunity for MillsonJames and HUB (née KuykendallGardner) to partner together again. He allowed me to make my sales pitch, and then he made a recommendation that I did not see coming: "Why doesn't HUB purchase MillsonJames?" My immediate reaction was to say no—an acquisition wouldn't make sense on many different levels:

1. MillsonJames' clients were HUB's competitors, so I anticipated we would be fired as soon as we announced an acquisition by HUB.
2. I loved what I was doing and didn't think I wanted to work for someone else.
3. It wasn't part of my plan.

These initial reactions were further cemented when I called my wife, Kristin, to tell her about my lunch with Chris. and she responded similarly, "Why would you want to sell and go work for someone other than yourself?"

Thankfully, like the statement I made as a twenty-two-year-old college student, we aren't held to our initial reactions or statements, and Chris continued to pursue the conversation. In following my father-in-law's advice and in keeping with my previous actions when faced with a potentially new venture, I confidentially reached out to friends and former colleagues who had sold their companies or had considered selling. Each of these discussions were instrumental in helping me make an informed and confident decision.

After much consideration and reflection, I agreed to sell MillsonJames to HUB International, and it served as one of the greatest decisions of my career. HUB provided me with new opportunities to learn and grow, and as has been the case throughout my career, I took note of these new opportunities and added many of these new experiences to my Reflection Collection.

During my time with HUB, I learned three of the most powerful words a leader can use are "I don't know." When Chris first approached me about the opportunity to be acquired by HUB, he requested that in addition to leading the MillsonJames business, I take on the role of president for employee benefits for the state of Florida. Upon hearing his plan, I strongly encouraged him to rethink that decision because I had never sat in the seat of those he was asking me to lead. I had always worked in and around the insurance industry but had never directly performed the role of an insurance broker. Chris's desire to have me join HUB and take on this new role was based more on my ability to lead people toward a common goal than it was about my institutional or market knowledge.

As a result of Chris's faith in me, I felt empowered to let go of needing to be the subject-matter expert on all industry matters. Responding to a team member's question with an answer of "I don't know" actually helped build a bridge of authenticity with my new team members. I worked hard to surround myself with people who possessed the answers and who felt empowered to use that knowledge to drive our business forward. This was an important lesson to learn and one that I'm thankful was part of my Collection.

After spending six and a half successful years with HUB International, I decided to call it a career, retire, and shift my passions into new areas, including writing this book. I have now dedicated my time to sharing my experiences, lessons, and reflections with anyone who will listen.

My career was filled to the brim with great experiences, incredible mentors, exceptional colleagues, and outstanding organizations. Whenever I have been asked what I enjoyed the most working for Hewitt, PlanSource, MillsonJames, or HUB International, my response was always the same—the people. As an extrovert, I am energized being around people. When I'm around people who share similar passions and seek a similar level of excellence, I flourish.

Lou Gehrig may have considered himself the luckiest man on the face of the earth, and who am I to debate my childhood hero for that title? However, I believe there is a distinct difference between good luck and good fortune. In my life and career, I lean more toward the latter. Being lucky means experiencing success by chance, without any control or effort, like winning the lottery. In contrast, being fortunate suggests a sense of gratitude for favorable circumstances shaped by our actions. Good fortune implies that we create our own luck through hard work and by diligently seeking opportunities to learn and grow.

Was it luck that one of my best friends from college, Chris Scheele, started working for Hewitt Associates a year before I accepted the same position, opening my mind to the possibility of joining such an elite organization? No, I believe it was good fortune, as I chose the people with whom I associated in college and worked hard to create the opportunity to interview with Hewitt. I was intentional about surrounding myself with individuals who pushed me to become a better student, communicator, negotiator, and leader. Even in my early twenties, I was tuning my frequency to learn from those around me, enhancing my chances of experiencing good fortune.

With all due respect to Lou Gehrig, I consider myself the *most fortunate* man on the face of the earth, mostly because of the people with whom I've shared this incredible journey called life. In finding the frequency of excellence, I was afforded the opportunity to learn lessons from some of the greatest mentors, leaders, salespeople, consultants, and communicators and for that I am eternally grateful.

And now I am more than happy to share those lessons with you in *Frequency of Excellence* in hopes that you can experience a similar level of good fortune.

SECTION 2

Professional Growth

CHAPTER 6

Seek Mentors—Build Your Own Reflection Collection

The people closest to me determine my level of success or failure. The better they are, the better I am. And if I want to go to the highest level, I can do it only with the help of other people. We have to take each other higher.

—JOHN C. MAXWELL

ONE OF THE more common misconceptions of mentors is that they must be formalized, or worse yet, sterilely assigned by an employer. This misconception limits the opportunity not only for growth, but also for the strength of a mentor/mentee relationship. As is true in life, relationships that develop organically are stronger and longer-lasting than those that are forced or artificially bonded.

From my first day at Hewitt Associates to today, I have been shaped by my colleagues—people with whom I have had the privilege to work alongside, managers who have challenged me, leaders who have led by example, teammates who have provided me with clarity, and friends who have held me accountable. Whether actively or passively, each of these colleagues have shared something special with me—a trait I found to be extraordinary. I have reflected on these situations, pasted them into my being, and they shaped who I am today.

Although I could have taken for granted the strength of the leaders for whom I worked over my thirty-four-year career, I credit one man for encouraging me at the outset to be on the lookout for excellence and to take full advantage of the leadership strengths that would soon surround me. It was my father who encouraged me to seek out mentors, watch them, and learn from them. It was from his own professional experiences that he learned the importance of mentorship and encouraged me to not allow the strength of others to pass me by without notice and without taking something unique from each of those experiences.

My father was clearly one of my most important mentors, and I called upon him frequently. He was my biggest fan and also my most honest critic. We would talk often about various business ideas and strategies, and I was in awe of his ability to quickly understand and dissect a complex concept. He would have loved watching the latter part of my career unfold. Unfortunately, my father passed away in 2009, so he missed the launch of MillsonJames, our growth, and, ultimately, our acquisition. In his absence, I leaned heavily on his early advice to seek out mentors and learn from their experiences.

A 2019 study from Olivet Nazarene University identified that 76 percent of American professionals believe mentorship is important, yet only 37 percent actually have a mentor.[3] This is both concerning and problematic, and I believe it is because too many professionals are looking for a formalized relationship, possibly one that requires an active opt-in/opt-out decision or maybe even a knighting ceremony complete with swords.

While some good can come from formalized mentor/mentee connections, I have found the best mentor relationships are ones that occur organically and informally over the course of working together. You may begin working with someone new and appreciate their leadership or management style. You may go to a meeting with an exceptional sales professional and walk away feeling energized by what you just witnessed. You may sit in the back row of a corporate town hall meeting and be impressed by the leader at the front of the room inspiring the attendees. You don't need to approach any of these individuals to formally ask for them to be your mentor. You simply need to pay attention, watch what they do, examine the decisions they make, and learn from them—tune your frequency. Over time, a relationship may develop; until then, just listen and learn.

I could list fifty-plus different mentors I've had over the course of my career, and in the vast majority of these situations, it was never a formalized or assigned relationship. I never had a mentor opt into this role, nor did I formally sit down with them to ask them to mentor me. In almost every situation, we simply began working together, and I found value in how they communicated, managed employees, or managed a client relationship. I became a fan of what and how they approached life, whether personally or professionally, and a relationship naturally developed. I carefully watched their actions and inactions, the decisions they made, and the results they obtained. I would then invest time to learn the rationale behind their actions—what data points did they lean upon to make their decisions? Why did they choose to do X versus Y? What outcome were they hoping to achieve? In these situations, when I found someone I truly admired or respected, I intentionally chose to become an engaged audience member in their career—watching, listening, and learning.

In the National Football League, we often marvel at the coaching trees of the league's greatest coaches. The coaching-tree metaphor has been used for decades to track the impact one coach has on the next generation of coaches. By working for and alongside legendary coaches and mentors, a younger coach has the ability to grow and develop, taking bits and pieces from those experiences and adding them to their own repertoire. A coaching tree is an exceptional way to track influence and mentorship throughout the NFL; it is also a very public example of reflective leadership.

Bill Belichick is widely regarded as one of the greatest NFL coaches of our generation (eight Super Bowl titles with the New England Patriots) and also has one of the most impressive coaching trees in the NFL. Throughout his illustrious career, he hired and mentored several exceptional future head coaches, including arguably the greatest college football coach of all time, Nick Saban (seven college football titles during his career as a head coach).

What I find fascinating is that while Nick Saban is a legendary coach in his own right, his career was clearly shaped by the mentors for whom he once worked. He is a reflection of his former bosses, most notably Coach Belichick. Through the various teams Nick Saban coached, he cut unique elements from his mentors and pasted them into his own being—how they interacted with their team, how they conducted training camp, how they structured their coaching staffs, how they treated the front office, or even the schemes they used to run their offense or defense. Coach Saban is crystal clear that much of what made him successful came from something he learned, saw, or heard from his mentors, specifically Coach Belichick. Coach Saban was clearly tuned in to his mentor's frequency of excellence.

Coaching trees are a wonderful exploration of genealogy and influence, as most every successful coach can point to a mentor for whom they once worked that helped them achieve their goals. Coach Belichick was mentored by a Hall of Fame coach in Bill Parcells and now Nick Saban has created his own far-reaching coaching tree that stretches across all of college football.

Regardless of industry, excellence is passed from leader to leader, mentor to mentee, as long as we are constantly observing and are open to growing.

Although I've clearly never coached a day in the NFL, my career was influenced greatly by my own version of a coaching tree. I am a product of the leaders with whom I had the honor and privilege to work over the years. Throughout my career, I can clearly point to an action or decision I've made as having learned it from something I heard, saw, or experienced with one of my mentors.

I am beyond fortunate to sit in the tree of some legendary professionals.

The beautiful thing about a mentor/mentee relationship is that as it develops organically, so does a genuine friendship that you can call upon throughout your lives. Throughout my career, I frequently have called upon my mentors when I have been faced with a difficult decision, a unique situation, or some form of a challenge. Because of the friendships that have developed over the years, those calls to my mentors are not only accepted but also handled with a great deal of care, love, and compassion.

Mentor/mentee relationships come in all shapes, sizes, and colors. They do not have to come from an employer/employee relationship and they don't need to fall within your chain of command. A mentor could be anyone you admire in your organization or community. They could be a leader at a local nonprofit where you attended a fundraising breakfast the year before. They could even be a parent of one of your children's friends. The fact is a mentor/mentee relationship knows no boundaries. A mentor can be any person in whom you find a skill, an experience, or a leadership trait admirable. It doesn't matter from where the person comes—it just matters that you have the desire to grow and you find someone you believe can help unlock the potential within you.

Finally, it is not lost on me that the majority of the business leaders under whom I worked were predominantly male. This is something that was clearly unintentional but was, rather, an unfortunate product of the time in which I entered the workforce—the late 1980s. I had the good fortune of being raised by a strong woman, married a strong woman, and we have raised a strong woman; however, during the foundational years of my career, the majority of my leaders were male. That said, I did have the privilege of working for and alongside some extraordinary female leaders including but certainly not limited to Gail Kellogg, Tilda Kaplan, Maureen Kincaid, Jocelyn Purtell, Linda Anderson, Maria Yao, Cheryl Fitch, Carrie Norden, Andria Herr, Angie O'Reilly, Deidre Guiseppi, Linda Keller, and Shelly Williams. Each of these leaders and mentors had a direct hand in helping shape my career, and for that, I am beyond grateful.

My encouragement for everyone, regardless of where you are in your career, is to identify exceptional people in your universe, watch them, learn from them, and include them within your own Reflection Collection. Don't sit back and wait—be active in learning and take mental notes of what you like (and possibly dislike) in how someone handles a situation.

Most importantly, when the time comes for you to be in a managerial or leadership position, be mindful of the fact that others are watching you and behave in a manner that would be encouraging, attractive, and inspiring. Serving as someone else's mentor is a privilege and I hope that you have the opportunity to serve in that capacity and become part of their Reflection Collection.

Mentorship is the key to unlock the power of future work generations.

CHAPTER 7

Address Your Fears Head-On (and with a Ulysses Contract)

> Do the thing you fear to do and keep on doing it. That is the quickest and surest way ever yet discovered to conquer fear.
> —DALE CARNEGIE

FACING A PHOBIA is never fun. Discovering a phobia in front of an audience full of college students is something I would not wish upon my worst enemy. Unfortunately for me, this is exactly when, how, and where I came to the realization I had developed a fear of public speaking.

During my fifth year at Hewitt Associates, I was asked to join the fall 1994 East Region Campus Recruiting Team, and I enthusiastically accepted their invitation. I had such fond memories of my own campus recruitment and was eager to share my passion regarding Hewitt with the students. Our first recruiting event that fall was at Villanova University. In addition to the candidates I was scheduled to interview, I had been asked to join other company representatives in delivering a presentation to all of the interviewing seniors the evening before. I was diligent in my preparation and showed no sign of hesitation or fear leading up to the event.

The Villanova emcee called each of the presenters to the stage and arranged us in sequential order for when we were scheduled to speak. I was excited and ready to wow the students with my wit, energy, and passion for Hewitt. As I heard my name called, I got up from my chair, walked across the stage, stood at the podium, and, in an instant, forgot pretty much everything I wanted to convey. My heart raced. Any moisture that was in my mouth went immediately to my palms as the former went dry and the latter sweated profusely. I froze as I watched a hundred-plus students stare right through me. It was unlike any feeling I'd previously encountered, and my racing heart sank into my stomach. I ultimately fought my way through the presentation, but as I returned to my seat on the panel, I was shocked and dismayed to learn I had developed a fear of public speaking. As upset as I was with my performance that evening, I was beyond uncomfortable with this newly formed glossophobia taking root and was determined to weed it out.

I returned from Villanova with a damaged ego and feeling a bit defeated, as I felt I didn't represent Hewitt in a manner that was commensurate with our stellar reputation. I did not care for this newly unearthed phobia, and I stewed on it for several weeks, trying to convince myself it was a one-time occurrence. Unfortunately, it was not, as I experienced a similar outcome at Rutgers University a few weeks removed from the Villanova gut punch. It was a similar situation with a similar outcome—dry mouth, racing heart, sweaty palms, and flushed face. I was disheartened but had this growing sense of renewal within me. The more I stewed on it, the more I knew I had to find a way around this obstacle.

Around the time of this struggle, I came across a comic strip that perfectly captured how my mind went haywire when I stood before an audience. Some of you may recall the comic strip *The Far Side*. It was written and illustrated by Gary Larson, and I quickly became a fan of his humor, wit, and unique perspectives on society; however, there was one particular comic that hit a little differently and very close to home. In this strip, Mr. Larson had Tarzan swinging through the trees of the jungle working to perfect his introductory lines for when he would first meet Jane. In the first few panels, Tarzan is practicing well-thought-out and perfectly executed lines such as, "How do you do? My name is Tarzan and I believe you are known as

Jane." The next panel is similar as he further practices his lines with, "Allow me to introduce myself. I am Tarzan, Lord of the Jungle. And you are...?" This continues as he swings through the jungle, right up until he sees Jane standing on a tree limb, swings to greet her, and blurts out, "Me Tarzan. You Jane." I could feel Tarzan's plight. His failure was in a tree in the jungle and mine was on university stages throughout the Eastern Seaboard. This particular comic strip spoke so clearly to me that I cut it out and taped it to my bathroom mirror. It became my daily reminder of the fear I was facing while also providing encouragement for my desire to overcome my newfound obstacle.

In the next meeting with my manager, Scott Bradley, I shared this newfound phobia and asked for his help and support. I asked him to look for opportunities to push me back up in front of groups and help me face my fears head-on. I needed to work through this obstacle. I gave him advance warning that I would stumble at times and some variation of "Me Tarzan! You Jane!" might spill out of my mouth. He understood and committed to provide me with opportunities to overcome my fears, which he did. I sought out opportunities to speak in front of internal audiences, to deliver client presentations, and address external audiences. There were some successes and some failures, but I learned a great deal from each.

Although it was nearly two decades before Ryan Holiday would publish his bestselling book *The Obstacle Is the Way*, I unknowingly attacked this newfound phobia with a similar resolve. I knew I needed to go through the obstacle to overcome it, and I needed to focus on things I could control. I realized I could not control how any audience would perceive me or whether they would appreciate my "performance." Instead, I turned my attention to the purpose of the presentation and how, as a member of the Recruiting Team, if I could convince one student that Hewitt was the exceptional employer that I found them to be, it would be a worthwhile endeavor. My focus shifted from being performance-based and, instead, became more purpose-based and served as a turning point for overcoming glossophobia.

Over time, I was able to overcome this fear, and now I have developed great confidence to stand in front of any audience and speak on a multitude of topics. I have been fortunate to have the opportunity to speak at regional and national conferences, sit on panels in front of hundreds of people, and have participated in live webcast events with thousands of people watching and listening. I can do this today because I identified a fear, developed potential solutions, and leveraged my community to help me achieve the success I desired. At the time, I didn't have a name for this, but I've since come to know this as a *Ulysses contract*, a commitment device that is rooted in Greek mythology.

A Ulysses contract refers to a decision or commitment made during a period of clear thinking that is intended to prevent impulsive or irrational behavior in the future. The term is derived from the legendary figure Ulysses (a.k.a. Odysseus) and a contract he made with his shipmates to save their collective lives. As you may recall from your junior high curriculum when you were required to read Homer's *The Iliad* and *The Odyssey*, Ulysses was on a return trip after winning the Trojan War. Their return voyage would have their ship pass near an island where the beautiful Sirens lived. Sirens were famous for singing melodious songs so beautifully that the sailors would get enchanted and so spellbound that they would wreck their ships on the rocks surrounding the Sirens' island. To overcome this obstacle, Ulysses asked his men to tie him to the mast of the ship and ignore any pleas he made to divert their voyage toward the island. He clearly knew his weakness and his inability to avoid a perilous fate on his own, so he enlisted the help of others and made a pact with them.

In a modern context, we use a Ulysses contract to outsmart our future selves. By approaching my manager, Scott, with a request to keep pushing me onto the "stage," I was creating a Ulysses contract that would prevent me from ignoring the truth of my phobia and to address it head-on. Scott helped me remain accountable to my goal of overcoming my fear of public speaking. Without it, I may have become numb to my discomfort and would never have improved my ability to effectively present in front of a crowd. With it, I am now able to stand up in front of any group and effectively communicate my message. Equally as important, I wasn't afraid of failure and had faith that for every time I fell off the horse, I would have an equal number of times I would successfully jump back on and attempt to gallop once again. I knew in my heart and had the support of my mentors, that I would eventually overcome the obstacle and conquer my fear—and I did.

This was a great life lesson for me to face my fears head-on and not waiver. It also served as a reminder for me to involve others in my plights and create some form of a commitment device to stop me from seeking an escape hatch and crawling through it. Overcoming the fear of public speaking wasn't easy, I can assure you of that—just ask any fall 1994 business school graduates of Rutgers or Villanova. However, with the support and guidance of others, it became much more enjoyable and feasible.

My encouragement for you is when you are faced with a similar obstacle, you find ways to face it and not avoid it, which is a central theme of Stoicism and *The Obstacle Is the Way*. The Stoics were clearly on to something as they faced pain and adversity with perseverance and resilience. They worked to turn every obstacle into an opportunity to get better, stronger, and tougher. One of the most famous Stoics, Marcus Aurelius, once stated, "The impediment to action advances action. What stands in the way becomes the way." Ryan Holiday does a masterful job of diving into this within his book, and I encourage you to read it to help you see your challenges as opportunities.

This may be the first piece of literature ever written that intertwined *The Far Side*, Tarzan, Greek mythology, and Stoicism in a single chapter, and there is probably a good reason for that.

Regardless of what method you use to overcome your obstacles, my hope is for you to simply do so—head-on and with the help of others.

CHAPTER 8

How You Do Anything Is How You Do Everything

We are what we repeatedly do. Excellence,
then, is not an act, but a habit.

—WILL DURANT

THE TITLE OF this chapter is a quote that has been attributed to various people ranging from Simon Sinek to Nick Saban, but I believe its true origin lies with Confucius. It is a short and sweet message that encourages us to strive for excellence in all areas of our lives, but in my opinion, it goes well beyond that. Whenever I have used this arrow from my quiver as a coach, parent, friend, and leader, it hits the bull's-eye every time.

The first time I heard someone utter this phrase was in the US Navy as I was learning to fold underwear, or skivvies, as the Navy liked to call them. I was in my second week of boot camp, and we were being trained on all things Navy, including how to make our beds, how to shine our boots, how to march in unison, and how to fold our clothes. Entering the Navy, I fully expected to be trained to make my bed a certain way as I had seen that exercise played out in countless military movies, and I was ready to bounce a quarter off my meticulously made bed. I also knew shiny shoes were distinctively military as was marching in a scripted formation. However, I recall being quite frustrated and maybe a little angry to learn there was a very specific way Uncle Sam wanted our underwear folded. It seemed crazy and over-the-top controlling.

It was during an evening meeting with our company commander, Chief Petty Officer Raymond Burroughs, when this assumed lunacy began to make sense. In an open forum, I asked Chief Burroughs why it mattered that we fold our underwear so specifically and precisely. His reply was simple and profound, "How you do anything is how you do everything." Being all of eighteen years old, I initially played along like I knew what he was talking about, but I didn't have a clue. Thankfully, he anticipated this and offered to dive deeper into the reasons why.

Chief Burroughs walked us through the preflight of a naval aircraft, the specific role each person on the team plays, and how critical it is that everyone pay strict attention to the details of their responsibilities. Precision is an absolute must in handling a multi-million-dollar aircraft. If someone on the team were to put forth a "good-enough effort" and miss a step in preflight, lives would be in danger. He then shared several other examples of how half-hearting a naval activity would be disastrous and, possibly, deadly. Those stories helped drive home the point that the Navy wasn't training us on how to fold underwear, but rather on how to do *everything* to the best of our abilities and with excellence.

This need for naval precision continued years later as I was trained to pick up trash. First, the Navy wanted to control my underwear folding; now they wanted to guide my trash pickup? Sheesh! Upon graduating boot camp in 1986, I was stationed at Naval Air Station Cecil Field in Jacksonville, Florida, to perform my reserve duties. I was assigned to VA-203, an attack squadron that flew the A-7E Corsair. At the beginning of each drill weekend, we would be called to muster on the flight line to perform a foreign object damage (FOD) walkdown—essentially, an organized trash pickup. Each drill weekend would begin the same; walking in a line with our eyes fixed on the ground. In this exercise, we would be encouraged to pick up any form of debris, no matter how big or small, because any foreign object that found its way into the jet engine intake of an A-7E would cause significant damage to the engine's rotors. Albeit mundane, this was obviously a critical task, and we were measured on our ability to clear the flight line of any and all debris. Oftentimes, there would be a second sweep by a more senior crew, and any FOD that was found in the follow-up sweep would be "highlighted," and there would be consequences for our inability to perform in the first FOD walkdown.

Once again, the Navy drilled home the importance of doing everything to the best of our ability, whether folding underwear or picking up trash.

As I progressed in my civilian career, as a leader, manager, and even as a parent, I adapted Chief Burroughs's words and tried to live my life according to a related credo: "Whatever you do, do it to the best of your abilities." I figured if I was going to invest my time in doing something, I may as well do it exceptionally well. There would be no half-hearted and good-enough efforts from me, and I would do my best to instill a similar belief in those I would lead, both personally and professionally. I am certain all my children would attest and likely roll their eyes that I continually encouraged them to do something to the best of their ability—mowing the lawn, studying for a test, washing a car, and so on. Not only would it help them strive for excellence in that particular activity, but also it would hopefully help them strive for excellence throughout their entire lives.

You should be aware that perceptions are formed by your colleagues and leaders in how you perform everyday tasks and projects. How you perform these tasks serve as an indication for how you might perform on larger, more important tasks. If your everyday emails are chock-full of typos and misspellings, your leader may think twice before promoting you into a client-facing position. If you continually show up late to meetings, your manager may question whether you have the sense of urgency that is required to lead XYZ project. This continual evaluation is often applied throughout an organization, and it starts with your initial interview. If your resume contains typos/misspellings, you can rest assured that either the interview will be short or may never happen. They will employ the "how-you-do-anything-is-how-you-do-everything" test, and if that is your best in trying to impress, trust me: they won't be.

Now, of course, there are limits to this. Winston Churchill famously once said, "Perfectionism is the enemy of progress." If you spend hours crafting an email because you want your points to be perfect, you've gone too far. If you find yourself excessively searching for new information to support a decision you need to make, you've fallen victim to analysis paralysis and will most certainly have limited any progress.

There is a fine line between perfect and excellent and we all need to be aware of where that line is. Striving for excellence should motivate you, not demoralize you.

The goal is excellence and the path to achieve it for you or your organization is to strive for excellence in everything you do, at all times. Half-hearted efforts will most always lead to half-hearted results. Be better than the person to your left and to your right on your version of a FOD walkdown. Excel at everything you do, and it will be noticed and recognized.

This lesson is a powerful reminder to continually adjust our radio dials to discover the frequencies of excellence around us, even when it seems a lesson is nowhere in sight. Folding underwear or picking up trash may appear simple and mundane, yet these tasks embody the principle that repetition fosters habits, and a habit of excellence paves the way to success. To put this into Chief Burroughs's parlance, when you habitually work to repeat excellence, even if it is in folding skivvies, the likelihood of achieving success increases dramatically.

CHAPTER 9

Poise under Pressure

We can complain because rose bushes have
thorns, or rejoice because thorns have roses.
—ALPHONSE KARR

A KEY TO REFLECTIVE leadership is the ability to keep your eyes and ears open and be constantly looking for learnings in everyday activities—tuning your frequency every moment of every day. Opportunities for growth come in all shapes and sizes and oftentimes they are right under your nose.

I have experienced several opportunities to witness poise under pressure throughout my career; however, the best and clearest example of this has lived and is currently living under our own roof—my twenty-four-year old daughter, Rose. As I write this chapter, Rose is lying in a hospital bed across from me in the neurology ICU awaiting a second brain surgery to combat a seven-year diagnosis of epilepsy. Since being diagnosed at age seventeen, Rose has demonstrated so much poise and grace while facing unfathomable adversity that it is difficult to not be in awe and even envious of her strength and grace.

As a parent, you never want to see your children suffer any ailment, particularly one that could potentially alter the trajectory of their lives. When Rose was first diagnosed, while we were trying our best to be strong for her and her siblings, I'm not going to lie and tell you it was easy. We were in a fog, trying to learn more about the condition, the limitations on driving, her ability to live alone, and the medications she would be taking to potentially reduce or eliminate the seizures. We called upon our faith and worked diligently to be strong for her and her siblings, but it was a struggle unlike anything we had ever faced.

That struggle was positively turned on its head for me on January 14, 2018. Rose had just experienced her second-ever seizure a few days prior and was in the midst of another round of MRIs, with a fair amount of poking and prodding. In the days that followed, our immense fog had returned, and we were struggling once again. Due to the enormity of the situation, Rose chose to stay home from school this January day and was sitting at our kitchen counter working on her computer as I entered the room. Upon walking past her, I caught a glimpse of her laptop's monitor, which read,

> Sometimes when things appear to be *falling apart*,
> They may be *falling into place*.

I was floored to read this. Blown away. Here I was in the middle of an avalanche of pity (for her and for us), feeling overwhelmed and struggling to piece everything together. I was confused, disappointed, anxious, and, at times, angry. Instead of joining me in a wallow of pity, she was sitting at our kitchen counter creating inspirational messages to hang on her wall. It was an unreal moment for me, and I had the wherewithal to grab my phone and discreetly take a picture over her shoulder to help never forget the day she provided me with such an incredible life lesson—a true gift.

Her poise under immense pressure was beyond my comprehension. Sometimes the lessons in our life are incredibly subtle, and we must finely tune our frequency to see or hear them. Other times, the lessons hit you squarely between the eyes and upside the head. This situation was clearly the latter and Rose's grace, composure, and poise were astonishingly inspirational and taught me a very valuable lesson in management and leadership—to find the positive even in the most challenging situation.

This memory came ricocheting back to me in 2023 as I entered my final year of professional employment. I was working for HUB International, and Kristin and I had agreed that I would retire at the end of the year to dive into some new passions and nonprofit work that had begun to stir within me. However, as I began to make plans to formally announce my retirement, I experienced several professional challenges that caused me to question whether it was the right time to retire. In addition to the professional challenges, I also experienced my own set of health challenges that served to only increase the speed of this 2023 mini-tailspin. It would be overly trite and a bit ironic to figuratively assume my heart was no longer in the business with retirement looming, but it literally was my heart that was beginning to fail. For factors that will never be fully known or understood, I was diagnosed with six different heart conditions mid-2023, which ultimately led to an expedited pacemaker implant surgery in September. All is well now, but with my heart issues layered on top of the newfound professional challenges, 2023 was quickly turning into one of the more challenging years of my life and career. I found myself wandering through an unfortunate but familiar fog. I was confused, disappointed, anxious, and, at times, angry—the exact feelings I had in 2018 with Rose's epilepsy diagnosis.

As I walked into this déjà vu moment, I was questioning the timing and the why behind what was occurring at work and with my health. Why were these situations happening? Could I have done anything to avoid them? What good would come through these trials? To say I was struggling and questioning a host of things would be a wild understatement.

Throughout my life, when my stress reaches an unhealthy level or I am faced with a difficult decision, I step outside. I have always found the outdoors to be healing and restorative, and fresh air helps me clear my mind, lower my blood pressure, improve my mood, and sharpen my focus. As I entered the fall of 2023 and as my personal and professional pressures mounted, I was in desperate need of some outdoor time. On one particular fall day, as I walked our dog around a beautiful and tranquil lake, I was struck with a memory that delivered the peace I was so desperately craving.

Sometimes when things appear to be *falling apart,*
They may be *falling into place.*

Just as Rose did in 2018, she helped me once again in 2023. I recalled the grace she displayed when faced with immense pressures, and it immediately changed my perspective, lowered my stress level, and I began to view things as falling into place versus falling apart.

We cannot control life's unpredictable challenges, whether they are health or career oriented. What we can control are our thoughts, attitudes, and responses to those situations. Perspective is a wonderful gift and can help you through the most difficult of times, but you must have the strength and resilience to call upon it.

In your life, when you find an inspiring example of someone displaying poise under pressure, I encourage you to make note of the situation, maybe even take a discreet photo, and file it away for your own rainy day. Those everyday examples are out there, you just need to have the desire and ability to tune your frequency to see and hear them. Oftentimes, they are right under your nose.

CHAPTER 10

Experiential Learning, Joy of Work, and Betty Crocker

I hear and I forget. I see and I remember.
I do and I understand.
—CONFUCIUS

'M NOT SURE what the equivalent of a clickbait title is in a book, but this chapter's title clearly serves a similar purpose. Just as it is when you come across an intriguing title while surfing the web or scrolling through your feed, you're going to have to read this entire chapter to understand how Betty Crocker's cake mixes of the 1950s apply to professional development today.

While attending UF and earning my bachelor's degree in business administration, it is safe to assume I didn't take a single class in which the Employee Retirement Income Security Act or 401k retirement plans were discussed or reviewed. As a result, when I graduated and signed on to join Hewitt Associates in their 401k/ Defined Contribution business unit, I was starting from a deficit position in terms of my knowledge of these retirement vehicles and had a lot to learn.

Upon my arrival at Hewitt, I found myself drinking daily from a firehose, having significantly more questions than answers and more client responsibilities than I likely deserved. Hewitt was well known for providing unique opportunities for younger associates, allowing them to participate and sometimes manage very large and complex cases early in their careers. We were encouraged to learn by doing. Hewitt believed that the perfect moment to grant someone more responsibility is before they were ready. For me, I was initially assigned a Fortune 500 client that was based in Atlanta; although I was certainly not ready, I did appreciate the opportunity to take ownership of a small piece of this client's service delivery.

A colleague named Brad Anderson was the senior consultant managing this large account to which I was initially assigned. As a result of my noted deficit position, I found myself repeatedly standing in his office, peppering him with a host of questions throughout the day.

Like an inquisitive four-year-old, my questions primarily began with how, what, when, where, and why. How do I reconcile these two reports? What does this mean? Where can I find that? If he was annoyed by my constant stream of questions (and he would have had every right to be), thankfully, he never showed it. However, as I've reflected on those first few months of employment with Hewitt, it wasn't Brad's absence of annoyance that stuck with me. Rather, it was the way in which he responded to my constant barrage of questions that served as a valuable lesson in coaching and has served me well throughout my career.

Brad understood that a key component of learning, particularly experiential learning, comes from the joy of experiencing it yourself. Rather than simply providing me with an answer that would have pushed me out his door sooner, he would take the time to coach and guide me to the resources that would provide the answer. For example, the recordkeeping system Hewitt was using at that time was a proprietary, batch-based system that processed employee retirement requests via fixed-file formatted transactions. To process a client's request, we would have to create unique batch transactions, all of which were detailed in eight to ten "blue binders" that sat on every consultant's bookshelf. With most any question I asked Brad, he would point me to the blue binders and tell me my answer resided in one of those two-hundred-page binders. With this guidance in mind, I would leave his office and begin my Sherlock Holmes-esque search for the answer.

If I'm being honest, I was initially frustrated by Brad's approach, thinking, *Wouldn't it be easier for both of us if you just told me the answer versus having me spin my wheels searching for it?* As I write this thirty-four years removed from those initial frustrations, I am so appreciative he did not simply provide me with immediate answers to my infinite stream of questions. Instead, Brad provided me with an opportunity to appreciate that experiential learning is a key to development and success. Not only was my ability to retain the new information dramatically increased, but I found joy in the work because I was fully engaged in understanding the hows, whats, whens, wheres, and whys behind it.

Which takes us back to the Betty Crocker "clickbait" chapter title.

General Mills launched a new line of cake mixes in the 1950s under the already-famous brand Betty Crocker. The idea was simple: the cake mixes included all the dry ingredients in the package, plus milk and eggs in powdered form. All the at-home chef needed was to add water, mix it all together, and place the pan in the oven to bake. For busy homemakers, it saved considerable time and effort, and the recipe was virtually error-free. General Mills had a sure winner on its hands—or so they thought.

Turns out despite the many benefits of the new product, it did not sell well at all. Even the iconic and trusted Betty Crocker brand could not convince homemakers to adopt the new product. After conferring with nationally recognized industry leaders and psychologists, General Mills determined the primary reason why the Betty Crocker cake mix struggled—it lacked the joy of work. The process to bake was *too simple*, and it didn't require people to get their hands dirty at all. Ultimately, people felt guilty serving a delicious cake that tasted homemade yet wasn't.

Brad must have known what the General Mills executives failed to initially understand: if something is produced too easily, you lose the joy of the work. Conversely, when you invest your valuable time to produce something, you gain a true sense of ownership. General Mills found this out the hard way as sales plummeted, and their product was headed toward abject failure.

So, how did General Mills solve this problem? They removed the powdered egg from the mix and asked the at-home chef to grab an egg from the refrigerator, crack it open, and add it to the powdery mix. In doing so, they engaged the homemaker in the process, and through one simple addition, the joy of the work returned. Sales skyrocketed, and the smell of freshly baked cakes, made with ease, filled the air. All because of a five-second, simple modification—just add an egg.

I have reflected on and mimicked Brad's style of coaching thousands of times over the years, and it hits the mark every time. As a coach and a leader, I deeply wanted to see my teammates succeed. I knew the best way for them to learn and retain information was to get their hands dirty and go looking through their version of blue binders for answers to their questions.

So, the next time you're coaching an employee, and they come looking for the easy answer—remember Betty Crocker and Brad Anderson and guide them to where they can find the answer, but allow them to do their own research and answer their own question. They will find more joy in their work, and the information will more likely be retained. If you make it too easy for them and you simply provide the coworker with the answer, they will more easily forget the information shared because they weren't actively engaged in the process—they didn't crack their own egg.

CHAPTER 11

Anything Essential Is Invisible to the Eyes

Be curious, not judgmental.

—TED LASSO

MY ENLISTMENT IN the US Navy didn't exactly follow a Hollywood script. Given that I came from three generations of US Naval Academy graduates and naval aviators, any childhood dream I had of joining the military were set aside when I opted against applying for an appointment to Annapolis. I figured I had lost any opportunity to be a part of my grandfather's Navy once that decision became final. However, who knew that I would be granted a second chance to follow in his footsteps, albeit from an enlisted sailor's point of view.

I was up against a financial wall and looking for a lifeline when my mother received that fateful call from a naval recruiter in 1986. I opted to return the recruiter's phone call for one reason and one reason alone—to solve a financial problem. I would not, on my own, have considered joining the Navy as an enlisted sailor/noncommissioned officer as that was never a dream of mine, nor was it a door I thought could be opened for a full-time college student. However, as I've noted before, my enlistment serves as one of the greatest decisions of my life as it opened a new world to me, exposed me to unique and powerful leadership experiences, and helped identify and deepen any form of grit that resided within me. With that decision and the experiences that followed, I demonstrated to myself that I would do whatever it took to be successful and make ends meet for my future family.

My enlistment began three days following the final exam of my freshman year at Florida. So much for a summer vacation. I took my Introduction to Shakespeare exam on a Thursday and boarded a Greyhound Bus bound for Orlando bright and early the following Monday. I had no idea what to expect but was soon to understand that the primary lesson I'd learn would be surprisingly unexpected.

Upon arrival at the Naval Training Center (NTC) Orlando, I spent the day running through a dizzying set of activities indoctrinating me to this new way of military life—receipt of military uniforms, gift of a fresh head shave, and the joy of owning my first pair of GI glasses, otherwise known as "birth control glasses" (BCGs). When I awakened the following morning, I was able to meet the eighty-three strangers who would soon become my friends and allies and form Company 116 of Orlando NTC.

The most striking thing about this first full day of basic training is how similar my new eighty-three friends looked—we all wore the same haircut, same clothing, same bewildered look, and for those of us with challenged eyesight, the same BCGs. The Navy had stripped us to our core, and their intention over the next 8.5 weeks was to build us back as sailors in the US Navy. It was a tremendous experience and taught me a great deal, but the single greatest lesson came from a place where I was not initially looking.

Our company consisted of young and grown men from all walks of life, from every corner of the United States, with myriad different life experiences. US naval boot camp is challenging, both physically and mentally, and its primary intent is to prepare recruits for the demands of naval service and weed out the weak minded. The drill instructors try to break you down and place you in challenging situations to ensure you're prepared for what may occur when you graduate and join the fleet.

From day one, we were encouraged and required to work as a team to achieve our daily tasks and challenges. This was no small feat given that we were working to harness unique skills and experiences of unfamiliar teammates. It was a once-in-a-lifetime experience and one that is difficult to replicate in a civilian world. However, the experiences and lessons learned through this difficult process were, in fact, surprisingly transferable, and I frequently have reflected on and applied these throughout my civilian career.

After the third week of boot camp, we began to form strong bonds with our shipmates as we learned to trust, respect, and appreciate each other for the qualities we brought to the company. There were no preconceived judgments of anyone since we had met for the first time just weeks prior. It was a special experience in that everyone was evaluated in real time based on what they brought to the table, how they treated people, how they led, and how they followed. Everyone's performance was truly measured on the results they helped the team achieve. Period.

Right around this same three-week mark, we began to receive letters from home, which lifted everyone's spirits. A new friend of mine was excited to receive a letter from his mother because she included some pictures from home. I had come to respect this fellow recruit because he and I had a similar set of values. He loved his family, was highly intelligent, and had a great sense of humor. However, as he shared his pictures with me, I felt an immediate pit in my stomach. Keep in mind I did not know this young man before boot camp and so I had no idea what he looked like in civilian clothes, with a civilian haircut, and with normal, civilian glasses.

As I looked at the pictures, I could not wrap my head around who this person was staring back at me through the photographs. What I saw was a long-haired, 1980s Ozzy Osbourne groupie with his mouth wide open and flashing the "rock-on" sign with his hands in pretty much every picture. I thought, *Who is this guy?* I convinced myself there was no way the young man in the photo was my new friend. To my temporary dismay, it was, and I now felt embarrassed. I shamefully admitted to him that I was glad I had the chance to meet him in the Navy because, had we met three and a half weeks earlier, my immature eighteen-year-old self may have judged him based on his outward appearance alone and walked the other way. While we were able to laugh about it, that unexpected experience taught me a great deal about life and people, and the lesson has stuck with me ever since.

It is in this unique naval experience I learned, firsthand and, luckily, at an early age, that you never judge a book by its cover. This lesson has served as such a strong and memorable reflection for me because of its startling and unique nature. I was blessed to have this experience in a contained environment like the Navy, where they stripped away all prejudgments and allowed us to formulate our opinions of people without traditional and societal filters.

What an amazing gift it was to have such an experience at a young age—an invaluable lesson to not judge others based on their outward appearance, be it the clothes they wear, the style of their hair, the glasses they choose to wear, or, most importantly, the color of their skin.

I never expected this lesson to be the gravy on top of my naval experience, but it clearly was, and for that, I am incredibly grateful. I wish everyone could experience diversity through a unique lens such as this. If that opportunity does not present itself, I share this reflection in hopes it causes others to suspend initial judgments and realize anything essential is invisible to the eyes.

CHAPTER 12

Et Loqueris Ad

Wise men speak because they have something to
say; Fools because they have to say something.
—PLATO

D EBATE IS A common occurrence in my family, and we
often have lively discussions on varied topics such as favorite food, favorite vacation, favorite Star Wars movie, or
favorite Harry Potter book. However, there is relative consensus
that the greatest sitcom ever created is *The Office*. Whether it is
the characters, the storylines, the dialogue, or the irreverence, we
love it, and we have collectively watched the entire series more
times than I'd like to admit.

One of my favorite scenes appeared in a season five episode ("The
Duel") in which Michael Scott, the lead character and bumbling
manager of Dunder Mifflin's Scranton branch, is taken aback when
his NYC-based boss asks for his advice and wants to know what
Michael is doing *right* at his branch. Given that Michael is better
known for being highly unprofessional and borderline cringy, he
ventures into new territory when he is asked to share his strategy for
recent sales success. With a smirk on his face, he begins to ramble,
filling the air with words and trying to be profound. As part of the
scene, Michael turns to the camera and says, "Sometimes I'll start
a sentence, and I don't even know where it's going. I just hope I find
it along the way. Like an improv conversation. An improversation."

Throughout my career, I have witnessed countless "improversations" and, unfortunately, participated in my fair share as well. I had kissed the Blarney Stone in Ireland and assumed I had been granted the gift of gab. I wrongly believed that as long as I was talking and was confident in my delivery, my audience would appreciate the improversation.

That belief changed for me in a small conference room in the Hewitt Associates' New Jersey office in 1995.

I had the honor and privilege to be working on a high-profile, high-revenue client, which was based in New York City. The team of consultants assigned to this account was a veritable Who's Who of Hewitt's East Region—consultants and partners who were exceptional at their craft. One of these consultants was Mark Arian, Hewitt's East Region legal consultant at the time. To help you appreciate the strength of this team, and using Mark as a proxy, he graduated from Duke University magna cum laude, received his JD from Columbia University, and was a partner at Hewitt. I, on the other hand, received my bachelor's degree just five years prior from UF and was a junior consultant trying to make my mark.

On this particular day, Mark and I were preparing for a client meeting in New York and were going over our talking points. Mark posed a hypothetical question to me and asked me how I would respond to the client. My response would have made Michael Scott proud—it was a perfect ten improversation. I filled the air with lots of words, thoughts, and ideas—some of which may have hit the mark, but there were far too many to truly understand what I was trying to convey.

Mark was very polite and an exceptional coach, so he allowed me to finish my soliloquy and then provided some much needed advice. He asked if I was familiar with the Latin phrase *et loqueris ad*. Given I had never taken a Latin class in my life, my response was, predictably, no. My response matched Mark's expectation and he began to share with me one of the most impactful lessons of my career. It was a true gift ,and I have tried to follow it every day since.

The translation of *et loqueris ad* is "speak with a purpose." Mark coached me on the importance of succinct communication and the significance of having a clear thesis to my words. He encouraged me to more actively listen, ask probing questions, take time to formulate responses, and then speak. Prior to receiving this advice, I often viewed conversation as a competitive sport, with the winner being whoever spoke the most words. Additionally, I would often attempt to respond to a client's query quickly, without asking any clarifying questions and likely not understanding the nature or purpose of their question. In these situations, my response would likely and unfortunately miss the mark.

What I learned through mentors like Mark is that our value is in the *purpose* with which we communicate, not the length or speed. Our words are valuable, and we should treat them as such.

Since being introduced to *et loqueris ad*, I have strived to follow three simple rules when communicating with others. I'm by no means perfect, as perfection is unattainable. However, I do strive for excellence in communication with others and have found these three rules to be immensely helpful for me in my career.

- Seek to fully understand the nature of a question. Ask quality and probing questions of the person who posed the initial question to you. Take your time. Be curious. *Be astonishingly curious.* The goal of most every conversation should be to listen more and speak less.
- Seek to fully understand the nature of the person asking the question. You must understand your audience. What are their drivers? What are their desires? What are their goals? Understanding your audience, especially if you don't know them in advance (e.g., an initial sales meeting), is a key to success. How do you achieve this if you've not met previously? Talk less—listen more.
- Be clear on the outcome you have in mind, yet be flexible. Whenever you enter a conversation or deliver a presentation,

you must be clear on the outcome you have in mind and ensure what you say, how you frame things, and the questions you ask are pointing you toward that desired outcome. That said, you must remain flexible because trying to achieve a predetermined outcome without first understanding your audience's goals and desires will most always yield a poor result.

Since that fateful day in a small New Jersey conference room, I have tried to speak more effectively and with a clear purpose. I reflect on this lesson continually when interacting with others. More importantly, I have tried to coach others to do the same and have worked diligently to model this behavior.

To quote Michael Scott, "My philosophy is basically this. And this is something I live by, and I always have, and I always will. Don't ever, for any reason, do anything to anyone for any reason, ever, no matter what, no matter where, or who, or who you are with, or where you are going, or where you've been. Ever. For any reason whatsoever..."

At the risk of trying to decipher Michael's wandering improversation, I believe what he was trying to say is this—speak with a purpose.

Et loqueris ad.

CHAPTER 13

Measure Twice, Cut Once

Prevention is better than cure.
—DESIDERIUS ERASMUS

MANY OF THE lessons I learned in my career immediately became part of my Reflection Collection while other lessons required multiple, self-inflicted missteps before they took root. This chapter's reflection was, unfortunately, most certainly the latter.

I was first introduced to the "measure-twice, cut-once" principle in 1988 during my summer employment with C&H Marine Construction. It was a great summer job and one that taxed me physically. We would work eight-plus hours a day in the Florida sun, carrying lumber, ripping plywood, and swinging hammers. Mark Stanley was my immediate supervisor and he had been with C&H for some time and was quite good at his job. However, it seemed his primary responsibility that summer was to physically toughen up the "college boys" who were assigned to his team—and he excelled at this part of his job. What he didn't realize was that in addition to toughening me physically, he sharpened me mentally as well.

Constructing anything requires a good bit of precision and planning. In our case, the architecture of the assigned dock, bulkhead, or boathouse had been carefully designed and planned by Ron Hendley, a Georgia Tech–trained engineer and the owner of C&H Marine.

Mark and Ron were an exceptional team—Ron would design; Mark would construct.

It was during this summer I first heard the phrase "measure twice, cut once," and Mark shared it liberally and loudly. I would frequently hear his booming voice travel across the water as I was about to cut a piece of wood: "Measure twice, cut once, Millson!" I had my fair share of errors, but Mark's encouragement for me to double-check my work saved a great deal of headaches, heartaches, and, most of all, precious lumber.

As I mentioned at the onset of this chapter, some lessons take multiple times to be taught and this is most certainly one of those.

Upon graduation from UF and as I began my professional career, I unfortunately lost sight of Mark's teaching and his booming voice had become a distant memory. I had to learn the hard way that measuring twice and cutting once is industry-agnostic and should be applied to any trade, any profession.

I could have used Mark's encouragement in 1994 while working for Hewitt in New Jersey. Our team had identified an overpayment error with one of our client's 401k distributions. Our resolution required us to reach for all affected participants to make them aware and kindly ask for repayment. I attacked the project with vigor, developed a corrective action, and quickly initiated the resolution—at least what I assumed to be the resolution. Turns out the program I developed to fix the error contained an error.

In my haste to quickly correct the issue, I exacerbated the problem. The letters we mailed to participants requesting reimbursement were incorrect. As a result, we had to mail a second letter, complete with a tail-between-the-legs apology. If only I had Mark shouting "measure twice, cut once, Millson!" in my New Jersey office as I developed the initial (incorrect) solution, we could have avoided the egg that clearly was headed for my face. Since that situation, I have repeatedly leaned into Mark's encouragement and have shared it liberally with the teams I led. Unbeknownst to him, Mark has saved hundreds of hours of rework and reputational hits across multiple businesses and industries.

In addition to the natural encouragement of double-checking your work to avoid costly errors, there are broader and inherent benefits to learn from Mark's lesson. Reflecting on this lesson has helped me be more measured, intentional, and meticulous in all aspects of my life—from relationships to communication and from financial decision-making to parenting. Essentially, Mark's principle is a timeless philosophy that promotes careful consideration, preparation, and attention to detail across all aspects of life. It encourages a proactive and thoughtful approach to decision-making and action, ultimately leading to more successful outcomes and fewer setbacks.

Although it took several missteps before this lesson became fully encoded in my brain, I'm grateful that it ultimately did. I'm thankful not only for his lesson but also for being tuned in to Mark's excellence on those hot and sweaty summer days. His encouragement to do things right the first time struck a chord with me in 1988 and became part of my Reflection Collection. When I call upon this memory, a smile comes across my face because Mark's Southern twang is clearly attached to it.

When you are next faced with a situation where you feel compelled to act quickly, my hope for you is, in whatever accent you speak or hear, that you hear a familiar voice encouraging you to "measure twice, cut once." Ultimately, when that voice causes you to slow down and take measure of what it is you're about to do or say, my further hope is you appreciate Mark's wisdom as much as I have.

As I began writing and researching this chapter, I was curious to know if Mark Stanley still worked at C&H Marine. Turns out, Mark passed away May 2020 after forty years of working at C&H. He ultimately became the owner of the company and oversaw a significant growth of their business, neither of which surprised me. I'm certain over the last several decades, there were countless employees who came under Mark's leadership that learned it is always best to measure twice and cut once.

CHAPTER 14

Be Kind Yet Truthful

Untidy truth is better than smooth lies
that unravel in the end anyway.
—GENERAL COLIN POWELL

I FIND IT INTERESTING how many of life's lessons can be taught
by the most unlikely of teachers and during the most improbable
situations. This fact is a good reminder that we should constantly
be aware of all that is happening around us and learn from all our
experiences, both in our personal and professional lives. This chapter's
lesson presented itself to me in a (somewhat) humorous manner, yet
has served me well in all aspects of management, leadership, and life.

The year was 1993, and I had just transferred from the Hewitt
Atlanta office to Hewitt New Jersey. My time in Atlanta was formative in many ways, particularly in the people with whom I had the
opportunity to work, the consulting experiences I gained, and the
skills I had begun to polish. However, one of the unforeseen skills
I picked up during my time in Atlanta was a fairly pronounced
Southern accent. Growing up in Florida (albeit North Florida), one
does not typically develop too thick of an accent, but if you spend a
few years in Georgia, it will most certainly put a drawl in your speech.
Therefore, you can imagine the looks I received when I arrived in
New Jersey where everyone thought I was as "country as corn flakes!"

At the time, Hewitt was still serving free breakfast and lunch to
their employees. Yes, this unique employee benefit was offered to

everyone during Hewitt's heyday—the privately held golden years. We had a full-scale kitchen at the office, and there was a staff who prepared and served us daily meals. Over time and quite naturally, we would develop relationships with the kitchen staff, and they would get to know us, our likes, and our preferences. In 1993, the woman who ran the Hewitt New Jersey Cafeteria was named Mo, and she was a real spitfire.

After a month or so, and thanks to my anti-*Sopranos* accent, most everyone had easily deduced I was not from New Jersey, including Mo. One morning she approached me with a giant smile on her face, generosity in her heart, and a warm bowl in her hands. She was excited to see me and presented me with a helping of freshly made grits. It was a very kind gesture because, as you could imagine, grits weren't a standard menu item in New Jersey. Because her effort was so extraordinarily gracious, I didn't know what to say other than "thank you," and to tell her how appreciative I was that she went out of her way to make me feel at home.

The issue was, though, I cannot stand grits. Never have liked them; never will like them. I would not eat them in a house, not with a mouse, not here, not there—not anywhere. So, I took my false appreciation and my grits to my office and sheepishly dropped them in the trash can.

Can you guess what Mo made me for breakfast the next day? The day after that and the day after that? She was excited to greet me each morning and present me with my freshly made bowl of grits, created especially for me. Given I had accepted them the first day without telling her the truth, I found myself perpetuating the lie day after day by politely accepting them, thanking her, and then returning to my desk and depositing them into my circular file. Thankfully, the grits production slowed and became more of a special occasion meal, but the fact still remained that I had not been truthful with Mo. As a result, I now carried this guilt, and she carried a well-intentioned burden of making grits that were being fast tracked to a New Jersey landfill.

This situation served as a unique management and leadership lesson for me as it spilled well beyond our New Jersey cafeteria. My initial inability to share the truth caused a great deal of unnecessary work and discomfort within an otherwise positive relationship. This unfortunately happens every day in people management and leadership. Often, a manager will feel they are doing the right thing by bypassing a performance issue and not addressing it directly for fear of disrupting the status quo. At the end of the day, when a leader fails to address the performance of an individual or a team, for whatever the reason, they not only have failed themselves but also have hindered the progression of the mission and the development of everyone involved. A leader may feel they are doing what is right by "being nice" or by "addressing it later," but this often leads to creating unnecessary work and discomfort within otherwise positive relationships, just as it did with Mo.

With the New Jersey grits memory at the forefront of my mind, I've tried to apply a reverse principle when managing employees—*how would I want to be managed?* Sort of the golden rule for management. Would I appreciate knowing something I've done incorrectly, or would I rather continue to perform at a suboptimal level because I wasn't aware it was suboptimal? Personally, as much as I might not want to hear the initial news that something I performed wasn't done as well as I may have thought, it beats the alternative of continuing to underperform in that area.

If I had applied this reverse principle in 1993, Mo could have saved a whole bunch of unnecessary time in the kitchen!

CHAPTER 15

Never Underestimate the Power of a Handwritten Note

While the spoken word can travel faster, you can't take it home in your hand. Only the written word can be absorbed wholly at the convenience of the reader.
—KINGMAN BREWSTER JR.

OVER THE LAST twenty-plus years, the television show *Survivor* has been a staple for our family. We absolutely love the show, and it has served as a true bonding experience for us. When our kids were younger, we would watch the show together and dissect the gameplay, personalities, and developing relationships. Now that our children have mostly grown and living on their own, we continue to watch it "together," texting one another throughout and following the show. Whether it is the strategic elements, social dynamics, or unpredictable twists, our family does not miss an episode, and we're constantly looking forward to the next. I've already had two of my adult children submit audition videos, and I'm fairly certain the trend will continue with the others.

One of my favorite episodes each season is when the remaining survivors receive handwritten letters from a loved one at home. The producers of the show use these letters to tug at the heartstrings of both the contestants and the audience. As the contestants read their letters, often aloud to tribemates and the cameras, you witness them break down in tears. The tears flow, not only because they are overwhelmed to receive something familiar from home, a place they have been longing to be, but also because they absolutely need the external encouragement within those letters to drive them toward the finish line. The power of those handwritten letters hits home every single time.

The producers of *Survivor* are brilliant in their design of the show, and they never allow it to grow stale. As a result, *Survivor* has been one of the longest running television shows in history. So many aspects of the show change from year to year—the number of contestants, the amount of food, the size of the tribes, the social makeup of the tribes, the challenges, and the rewards. However, one of the main constants throughout all forty-six seasons has been the handwritten note from home. The producers understand the incredible power of a handwritten note.

Handwritten notes have held a unique and powerful significance throughout the history of our country. Whether it was Dr. Martin Luther King Jr.'s letter from Birmingham Jail, John F. Kennedy's Cuban Missile Crisis letter to Nikita Khrushchev, or Jim Halpert's handwritten note in the teapot to Pam Beasley, handwritten letters are powerful in evoking emotions and are uniquely persuasive in achieving their outcomes. Now, of course, in the years prior to the turn of the millennium, the primary form of communication was, by default, handwritten. However, even in today's world of superconnectivity and omnipresent electronic communication, the power of the handwritten note remains absolute and persuasive.

The immense power of a handwritten note lies in several unique aspects of this form of communication. First and foremost, it is highly personal because the person who wrote it permanently stamped it as their own by using their distinctive penmanship. It can never be replicated, unlike every other form of digital communication today.

Secondly, and equally as important, the physical act of writing and receiving a handwritten note creates a true connection between sender and receiver that is impossible to replicate digitally. The effort put into crafting a handwritten note enhances the emotional impact upon receipt because the receiver truly appreciates the time, care, and consideration the sender took to craft it. This demonstrates a commitment that goes beyond the convenience of its digital cousin.

Finally, the element of surprise and delight in receiving a handwritten note cannot be overstated. In a world dominated by digital communication, receiving a handwritten note can evoke intense and positive emotions, including a nice shot of dopamine. Indeed, the fact that there are so few handwritten notes sent or received these days is the very reason why the feelings are so positively intense when you receive one.

Over my career, I have witnessed countless examples of the power of a handwritten note. It is one of my more powerful reflections, mostly due to how the memory is tied to sincere, positive, and strong emotions. A handwritten note of thanks to a colleague, a quick word of encouragement to a teammate, or some form of handwritten praise will be appreciated by the receiver 100 percent of the time. It never misses and often the appreciation can extend well into the future.

I experienced this delayed gratification when I announced my retirement on LinkedIn. As I shared the news of my downshifting into new passions and projects, I heard from friends and former colleagues, many of whom I'd not heard from in years or decades. It was nice to hear from everyone, but there was one particular response that further drove home this lesson of the power of the handwritten note.

Hewitt had hired a woman named Jody VanArnam (née Pelfrey) in 1997 when we first opened the Orlando office. It was evident from day one she would have a long and successful career as she hit the ground running, making her value instantly obvious. Well, apparently, at some point in her first few years with Hewitt, I wrote her a note to thank her for something she'd done well and to encourage her to keep up the good work. I don't specifically recall the note, but she certainly did, taking the time to respond to my retirement post with this message. She wrote, "I still have my handwritten card from you early in my career that was very heartfelt and specific of what you were thankful for with me. I have always carried that forward...

thanking people personally and specifically. A personal message goes a long way." The beauty of this lesson is that I was not even aware my handwritten note meant so much to her, so much so she kept the card for nearly twenty-five years! Equally as impactful was the fact Jody carried and paid forward the power of the handwritten word with her team over the last twenty-five years. Her LinkedIn message was powerful for me and affirming for this lesson.

The second lesson I'd like to share demonstrates the power of the handwritten note in the recruitment process. Within the last year, my daughter was introduced to someone in our community who was actively looking to fill an open position on her team. The owner of this company is a bit of a celebrity in our town, having published her own cookbook and appeared on several TV shows. This was a coveted position, and Rose was very excited for her interview. Following the interview, Rose was anxious to hear from the owner/ decision-maker. In the meantime, some good friends of ours, Alex and Daryl Place, who were involved in initially introducing Rose to this opportunity, asked if she had sent a follow-up and handwritten note to the owner. She had not, yet appreciated the suggestion, and quickly grabbed a pen and notecard to send a heartfelt, handwritten thank-you note. Within a week, she received the good news that she had been selected for the position. Since that time, we have been told by countless people who are close to the owner that Rose's handwritten note was the deciding factor. As a hiring manager, I have always appreciated and made note of any handwritten thank-you note I've received, and apparently, so did our celebrity chef.

Finally, I have also witnessed the power of the handwritten note in sales situations. I've worked with several exceptional salespeople who consistently made it a point to send a handwritten note to a prospect as a way to thank them for their time and share appreciation for the opportunity to earn their business. For all the reasons noted above, when a buyer receives a handwritten note, they feel a connection with the salesperson, and they recognize and appreciate the extra effort it took to write a personal and handwritten note. That shot of dopamine felt by the buyer could be the difference between a win and a loss.

If we're being honest, every good salesperson sends a follow-up email to a buyer. A follow-up email has become table stakes in today's marketplace. The problem is the digital thank-you can quickly become white noise and lost in a sea of a hundred emails the buyer may receive that day. However, if you, as a salesperson, take the time to send a handwritten note, I can assure you it will stand out, and your close ratio will increase. Selling is not easy, but sending a handwritten note is. I highly encourage you to invest the five minutes it takes to send a heartfelt and handwritten follow-up note. You'll be glad you did.

Every day we are bombarded with ways to make life more efficient and streamlined—as a leader, candidate, or sales professional. We are constantly trying to find more time in our days. Writing a handwritten note feels so 1900s and inefficient. I cannot argue against either of these points. However, what I can argue and have scores of examples to support is that a (seemingly inefficient) handwritten note will evoke significantly stronger feelings and will stick with someone much longer than an (efficient) email or DM.

The real question for you: Do you want to be more efficient or more effective? As it relates to communication, I hope the answer is clear and you feel encouraged to pick up an old-fashioned pen and paper to thank, appreciate, or connect with someone.

As they say in *Survivor*, the tribe has spoken.

CHAPTER 16

Engage Deeply in Professional Exploration—Wisdom Quest

The journey of a thousand miles begins with one step.

—LAO TZU

FOR TOO MANY, the word "in-law" unfortunately sends shivers down the spine. The movie industry has made millions of dollars by highlighting the dysfunctional relationships that exist between sons-in-law and their wives' parents. Additionally, therapists around the globe have worked tirelessly to help both sides of the in-law equation identify ways to not tear each other apart at Thanksgiving dinner. Fortunately for me, I was blessed with my assignment of in-laws, as I love and have a great deal of respect for all sides of the in-law equation: brother, sister, mother, and father. I feel like I won the in-law lottery—particularly as it relates to my father-in-law, Dr. H. Russell Fogler.

Russ is truly one of the smartest people I've ever known, with an undergraduate degree from University of Pennsylvania and advanced degrees from both University of Michigan and Columbia University. He taught University of Florida students Quantitative Methods of Business and Finance classes for well over a decade, including my older brother (thankfully, he retired the year before I took QMB at UF). However, as intelligent as I believe Russ to be, it is his wisdom that I appreciate more than anything.

When I first married Russ's daughter, he shared various pearls of wisdom with me, many of which became part of my Reflection Collection. The first pearl was to always have two years of salary set aside in savings, which served me well when I founded MillsonJames. The second was that you should read at least two books written by authors who have experienced something that you'd like to begin to master. For example, when I joined Hewitt Associates' e-business (Sageo) in 1999, I quickly sought out and read several books on e-commerce and e-customer care to help me learn more about this emerging trend called the internet. (Apparently, in the late 1990s, if a business or service was associated with the internet, we threw an *e* in front of it.)

This latter encouragement from Russ to seek out knowledge from people who have had success in a particular realm has become a large part of who I am today. I rarely tackle a new endeavor or make a critical, career-altering decision without seeking advice and counsel from experts in that field. Whether I'm meeting with someone live or reading their book, the desired outcome is the same: to become more educated and learn from their successes and challenges. More specifically, I want to understand their thought processes, what led them to make certain decisions, how they avoided (or not) certain land mines, and how they grew their knowledge and became an expert in their field. I have initiated this process well over a hundred times throughout my career and several of these engagements are detailed within these pages. I so firmly believe in this form of education and knowledge seeking that I will continue this for the remainder of my life. Indeed, as I contemplated retirement and even considered writing this book, I reached out to friends, former colleagues, and some of my favorite authors to learn about retirement as well as the ins and outs of authorship. I have ultimately come to refer to these interviews as a Wisdom Quest.

The true value of a Wisdom Quest is not in *how many* experts you engage, but just that you do engage. There should be a direct correlation between the number of experts to whom you reach out and the magnitude of your potential decision. For rather simple decisions or considerations, you can likely get smarter on a subject by speaking with a rather small handful of people. However, for larger, life-altering decisions, I would highly encourage you to meet or speak with as many experts as are willing to meet with you. For example, when I was considering launching MillsonJames, I must have met with fifteen different entrepreneurs and business owners to pick their brains and learn from them. This was a massive decision, as I was contemplating leaving an executive position with a growing organization to launch my own firm with a starting compensation of exactly zero dollars. So, yes, this was a rather large decision and, therefore, my Wisdom Quest was of correspondingly similar size. For the MillsonJames Wisdom Quest, I can say that without fail, I left each of those meetings smarter than I was the hour before.

I do offer one bit of caution as it relates to a Wisdom Quest—do not fall victim to analysis paralysis. At some point, a decision must be made, and you cannot use the quest to kick the can down the road and delay a decision. I have found that tapping into an expert greatly enhances a decision-making process, but there comes a point where you must use that information gained to make an informed and final decision. You must decide whether you are going to fish or cut bait—and then do so.

By and large, there are six primary objectives I set when I launch a Wisdom Quest with a goal of hopefully increasing the odds for a successful outcome.

1. SPECIALIZED KNOWLEDGE OR EXPERIENCE: My outreach to an expert or my decision to read a certain author's book is primarily based on my desire to learn from someone smarter than me on a particular and specific topic. That individual has specialized knowledge or experience that I do not, and I would like to learn from them.

2. **DIFFERENT PERSPECTIVE:** I often approach these discussions with a certain viewpoint in mind. My desire to speak with an expert or read their book is intended to help me gain a new perspective. As with anything in life, when you look at something from a different angle, you see it entirely differently. These Wisdom Quests offer me a new perspective.

3. **VALIDATION OR INVALIDATION:** As humans, we are constantly looking for validation and a Wisdom Quest may very well offer you that outcome. However, you should enter into the discussion with an open mind, understanding your initial assumptions may actually be invalidated. Either way, you leave the discussion or put the book down with more information than you had prior to engagement and are better for it.

4. **RISK MITIGATION:** Engaging with an expert helps identify and mitigate potential risks associated with a decision or action. Their expertise enables you to foresee challenges and propose potential strategies to avoid, manage, or overcome them.

5. **PROFESSIONAL GROWTH:** Diving into a topic with an expert can help you maintain a continuous growth mindset. Learning from those who excel in their areas of expertise can enhance your own skills and knowledge base, making you better equipped to tackle not only the current decision before you, but also future decisions.

6. **EXPANDING YOUR NETWORK:** As you engage with the expert, you are not only learning from them, hearing a different perspective, validating your assumptions, mitigating risk, and growing, but you are also expanding your professional network and, possibly, gaining a new mentor.

I can say with 100 percent certainty that every Wisdom Quest I've executed has left me smarter than when I initiated it. Whether my initial assumptions were validated or invalidated, I was better off for the exploration.

My father-in-law's wisdom is as appreciated today as it was back in 1990 when it was first shared. Russ's simple suggestion of reading two books on a subject I'm interested in pursuing led me to create my own version of the Wisdom Quest, and it has served me incredibly well.

When you are faced with career-altering decisions or are contemplating a new endeavor, I highly encourage you to identify the experts you can call upon and from whom you can learn. Thankfully, in my case, the original expert that I engaged happened to be sitting across from me at a very peaceful Thanksgiving dinner.

SECTION 3

Management

CHAPTER 17

Feedforward > Feedback

A good coach will make his players see what
they can be rather than what they are.

—ARA PARSEGHIAN

A LTHOUGH I BELIEVE firmly in the need for people to be
on a constant learning journey, I am not what you might
formally call a career student. When I graduated from UF
in 1989, I was ready to move on and did not ever want to sit through
another exam or write a paper for a grade. Even though I had considered myself a good student, I had hit my limit in terms of formal
schooling and was ready to enter the School of Hard Knocks with its
own brand of experiential learning. Unlike my father, father-in-law,
or wife, I knew an MBA, PhD, EdD, or any advanced degree for that
matter was not in my future, but I also knew that for me to advance
my career, I would have to be in a continuous learning mode.

Thankfully for me, my initial employer also believed in continuous
learning and pushed us to be in a constant state of development.
We were frequently encouraged to seek out training that would help
us develop and improve ourselves as both consultants and leaders.
Over my seventeen-year career with Hewitt, I was afforded the
opportunity to take a multitude of training courses that helped me
develop skills I felt were lacking or needed additional polish. Within
these Hewitt years, I can clearly point to a large handful of training
courses that left an indelible mark on me and upon which I reflect

and lean continuously. The impact of these Hewitt training courses was so significant in my development I kept many of the hardcopy materials, and they sit on my office bookshelf today. One of those binders contains materials from a 2003 Hewitt leadership training event that first introduced me to a groundbreaking management concept that I have utilized ever since.

The facilitator of this leadership training was a gentleman by the name of Dr. Marshall Goldsmith, who at the time, and still is today, one of the top executive coaches in the world and was recently inducted into the Thinkers50 Hall of Fame. It was during this leadership event I first learned of the key differences between "feedforward" and feedback. The introduction of feedforward changed the way I managed people forever, and I have shared Dr. Goldsmith's wisdom hundreds of times over.

It has been said by countless people that "feedback is a gift," and it generally rings true. Successful businesses rely on open and honest feedback between coworkers, and those same businesses require their leaders to seek out and deliver feedback as well. So, if there is such a preponderance of evidence that supports the value of feedback and that it should be provided and received as a gift, why does hearing the word *feedback* tighten stomach muscles and create significant anxiety within people?

The reason, as I learned in 2003 from Dr. Goldsmith, is because there is a fundamental problem with feedback: it focuses on the past, on what has already occurred, and it often leads to defensiveness upon receipt, no matter how constructively the feedback is shared. It matters not whether the feedback is positive, negative, constructive, or destructive, feedback focuses on behaviors someone previously exhibited and there is nothing the receiver can do to change the outcome or perception of those formerly exhibited behaviors.

The idea behind feedforward is that it provides guidance, coaching, and suggestions to an individual for events that have not yet occurred, and it strips away any potential or natural defensiveness that often is associated with feedback. For example, imagine how it feels to receive feedback on how poorly a sales pitch went versus receiving feedforward coaching on ways to deliver a future pitch. The former likely produces the aforementioned tight stomach, and the latter gets the adrenaline pumping. Said differently, feedback is often received as judgment, while feedforward is received as coaching.

As Dr. Goldsmith laid out for us in that training event and as adapted from his article written on the same topic, the top reasons why someone should utilize feedforward versus feedback are as follows:[4]

- We can change the future. We cannot change the past. Feedforward helps people envision and focus on a positive future, not a failed past.
- It is more productive to help people be right, than prove they were wrong. Constructive feedback often is negatively received because it focuses on mistakes, shortfalls, and problems. Conversely, feedforward is almost always received positively because it focuses on solutions.
- Successful people appreciate coaching that is aimed at helping them achieve their goals and resist negative judgment that is often felt by feedback.
- People do not take feedforward as personally as feedback. Whether intentional or not, developmental feedback is almost always received at a personal level. Feedforward cannot involve a personal critique since it is discussing something that has not yet occurred.
- Feedforward reinforces the possibility of change and success whereas feedback may reinforce the feeling of failure.

Although there have been hundreds of coaching sessions in which I've deployed this principle, there is one particular situation that often comes to mind when I reflect upon the utilization of feedforward. The first consultant I hired at MillsonJames was a woman by the name of Margaret Godwin. Margaret and I had worked together at

Hewitt Associates for several years, and I always respected her for her energy and passion for serving clients.

Upon her arrival at MillsonJames, she spent the majority of time watching, listening, and learning how we consulted with our clients. Her learning curve was steep, but she was making solid progress, and it was time to provide her with the opportunity to lead her own consulting project, one in which she would be in the driver's seat and I would be riding shotgun. She did a great job with the customer and was eager to receive feedback on how she performed.

The following day we sat down to debrief her consulting performance. Before we met, I reflected on Dr. Goldsmith's feedforward principle and opted to deliver my comments in his prescribed manner. We talked about her future projects and different ways she could go about her questions and follow-up. We dissected different ways to ask probing questions and to gather the necessary information that would serve as the basis for her downstream consulting. The meeting couldn't have gone better, and Margaret was uplifted and ready to tackle the next project.

By framing the coaching session in a feedforward manner, Margaret received the information positively, and it reinforced the likelihood of success. If I had provided the information via feedback, she may have been defensive, and my coaching may have reinforced a feeling of defeat and failure on her maiden consulting voyage.

Feedforward for the win!

Thankfully for me and the teammates I coached over the years, I was tuned in to the right frequency in 2003 during the Hewitt leadership training event. I was so moved by the idea of feedforward that I decided to immediately begin utilizing this new management technique and excitedly added it to my Collection.

I'll share some encouragement with you within a feedforward frame—I would strongly encourage you to dive deeper into this concept of feedforward by reading some of Dr. Goldsmith's articles on the subject. It is a powerful tool for all managers and coaches.

Trust me: you will appreciate having this new item added to your own Reflection Collection, and you will use it liberally.

Feedback is a timeless gift to give. However, if you truly respect and appreciate the person to whom you are providing this gift, I would highly recommend you swap it out for a gift of feedforward.

CHAPTER 18

Be Slow to Hire
(and Remove Beer Goggles)

*Don't make the same decision twice. Spend time
and thought to make a solid decision the first time
so that you don't revisit the issue unnecessarily.*

—BILL GATES

IME IS A fickle and funny thing, particularly when it comes to management and recruiting—too little of it on the front-end of an employment relationship and too much of it on the back end can be devastating to an organization. Given that people are an organization's single greatest asset, it is imperative, as a manager and leader, that you do not invert these two sets of time investments.

Unfortunately, the following tale is repeated daily throughout all businesses across all industries: Someone approaches their manager about an open recruiting need, and they passionately state how critical it is the manager backfill the position as soon as humanly possible, or the team simply cannot operate without replacing {John or Jane Doe} immediately, or the business will come to a screeching halt if the manager does not find a replacement ASAP!

Sound familiar?

In the world of recruiting, the need to backfill a position is often not in doubt. However, the need to find the *right* person should be absolute and should trump any stated need for speed. Unfortunately, the real or perceived pressure to promptly backfill often creates a mirage effect for the hiring manager. This mirage effect is the re-cruiting equivalent of professional beer goggles—candidates begin to appear more attractive because of the perceived pressures of quickly filling an open position. When this occurs, hiring managers tend to overlook obvious shortcomings—previous job-hopping, limited experiences, questionable communication skills—to quickly fill the open seat.

The perceived need to hire someone quickly is a powerful force if left unchecked. As a leader, it is imperative you see through this mirage and encourage the team to take a deep breath, suspend short-term desires, and focus on finding the right candidate to achieve sustained results. In general and in recruiting, it is the responsibility of a leader to always maintain focus on the long term.

There are a host of studies that estimate the financial costs of hiring the wrong employee, but the collateral damage of hiring an ill-advised person extends well beyond the financial realm—it can affect employee morale, company culture, and even the company's brand. Given the long list of potential challenges, in the world of recruiting, when faced with an "urgent-vacancy-that-must-be-filled-immediately" request you must take a deep breath, pump the brakes, and settle in for a thorough recruiting process to run its course.

Essentially, you must be focused on finding the right candidate slowly versus the wrong candidate quickly.

On the other side of the employment spectrum, and we have all fallen victim to this, there is a strong tendency to drag out the termination process even when it is crystal clear to all involved that a toxic employee must go. Whether it is our human instinct to want to fix a problem, a tender heart, or the concern of further reducing staff on an already stretched team, a termination process is often and unfortunately measured in months or years, not weeks. Now, to be perfectly clear, I am not suggesting HR processes should be circumvented and employees should be fired willy-nilly without cause. However, assuming the appropriate management, HR, and legal processes are followed and documented, I have learned it is better for everyone involved to expedite the termination process when you've determined it is clearly time for someone to depart. The return on energy expended will never be positive and it typically ends up in elongating the inevitable—wasting both precious time and money and, equally, if not more important, negatively impacting the culture of the organization. There is an axiom I have reflected upon in these situations and it comes from Jeremy Foley, the retired athletic director at the University of Florida, who famously once said, "What should be done eventually must be done immediately."

Although I had experienced both of these scenarios throughout my career, the lesson of being "slower to hire" was on constant display in working with Chris Gardner, CEO of HUB International Florida. Chris continually encouraged and held us accountable to take our time and find the right candidate. There was one particular hiring process that perfectly illustrated the benefits of not allowing the urgency of a hiring situation to lower recruiting standards.

In this situation, HUB Florida had been looking, ironically, for an in-house recruiter for well over a year. Throughout the process, we interviewed a slew of candidates, and while we got close to hiring a couple of different candidates, we never could quite get comfortable. There was always some nagging nuance that caused us to hit the pause button and continue looking—job hopping, incongruent compensation requests, gaps in resume, and so on. The further we got into the process, the urgency to fill the position only increased. Managers were feeling desperate, as was the hiring team—the beer goggles were coming out in full force. However, with Chris's voice ringing in all our ears (quite literally since he was heavily involved in the process), we took our time, didn't lower our standards, and ultimately found an incredible candidate. Had we prioritized speed over quality and looked past identified concerns, we very likely would have made a mistake and been back to square one within a matter of months. Instead, we took our time and found the ideal candidate who filled the role perfectly and performed masterfully.

Recruiting is a beautiful combination of both art and science, and you should lean into both as you're looking to fill open positions. The artistic side of recruiting comes in the form of understanding the candidate's fit within the organization or their Wayne Gretsky–oriented potential (foreshadowing for the next chapter). The science comes in the form of understanding that a candidate's past employment patterns are strong indicators of future behavior. Don't overlook science and go entirely with art. Conversely, don't allow a process to be overly scientific and resume-based.

Most importantly, recognize that neither art nor science can be rushed.

Although Bill Gates was not necessarily referring to recruiting when he made this comment, it perfectly sums up this lesson and is worth repeating:

> *Don't make the same decision twice. Spend time and thought to make a solid decision the first time so that you don't revisit the issue unnecessarily.*

CHAPTER 19

Be Like Wayne [Gretsky]

What lies behind us and what lies before us are
tiny matters compared to what lies within us.
—RALPH WALDO EMERSON

W E ARE TOO often wowed by a candidate's resume—
someone who has all the requisite skills and experience:
attended great schools, worked for outstanding employers, and has exceptional experiences. On paper, they appear
to have all the right qualities and attributes. In college-football-recruiting parlance, they are the quintessential "five-star recruit" and
a "can't-miss prospect." Like many others, I have at times assessed a
candidate based on their past experiences, akin to looking at their
candidacy through a rearview mirror. However, my perspective was
forever changed during my involvement in a hiring process in the
early 2000s. That situation prompted me to begin assessing candidates based on their forward-looking potential and viewing their
candidacy through the front windshield.

I was fortunate to be part of the leadership team to open the
Hewitt Orlando office in 1997, and I was excited to return to my home
state. Joe Bialek had been selected to lead the office, and I had the
pleasure of getting to know Joe as we had worked together in New
Jersey. Joining us was a woman from California whom I had not yet
had the opportunity to meet as she had been working on-site with
one of Hewitt's larger clients on the customer service (CS) side of

the business. Her name was Cheryl Fitch, and she was a rising star in the CS business unit.

Within five short years, the Hewitt Orlando office had grown to nearly two thousand employees and we were providing services that stretched beyond our initial call center services, including technology, administration, and broader consulting. An opportunity came available for Hewitt to fill a senior position (business group manager—BGM) with P&L responsibility and management of a broad set of Hewitt's services. At that point of Hewitt's history, most every BGM throughout the firm was promoted from within and came from the technology/administration/consulting side of the business, not CS. There was certainly no written rule about this, but it was how things had played out over the years.

When the Orlando BGM position became available, there were several strong candidates from which to choose, and it was not an easy process. Several candidates from the technology/administration side of the business had tossed their hat into the ring, as did Cheryl. It was this particular hiring process that made me reflect on a famous quote from Wayne Gretsky (NHL Hall of Famer, a.k.a. the Great One), when he said, "I skate to where the puck is going, not where it has been."

The decision to hire a BGM would have been much easier if we had stuck to tradition and looked only at where the candidate's puck had been (past technology/administration experience and expertise). As noted in the previous chapter, relying solely on this would have been overly scientific and short-sighted. Instead, the hiring committee looked at where the puck was going for the candidates and assessed their *potential* as part of the decision-making process.

In the end, Cheryl received the promotion and became one of the strongest BGMs at Hewitt and ultimately led the east region for Hewitt's outsourcing business. She retired a few years ago after serving in various leadership capacities and leading Alight's (née AonHewitt, née Hewitt Associates) largest outsourcing client. If Hewitt's leadership/recruiting team focused solely on where the puck had been with Cheryl and only saw her CS background, we would have missed the opportunity to capitalize on her innate leadership abilities in a much broader manner, and she wouldn't have had the opportunity to lead and inspire so many people over the years.

A few years ago, I read a story about Super Bowl LII and how many of those players were three-stars or below coming out of high school, and I was blown away. Before diving in, allow me to provide some context for anyone not overly familiar with college football recruiting. Coming out of high school, each recruit is assigned a star rating from zero to five, with five stars being the highest and most heavily recruited. Five-star recruits have incredible resumes and check all of the right boxes (height, weight, speed, etc.). A highly average two- or three-star prospect doesn't have a great looking resume, or they lack certain skills or attributes. At the other end of the five-star spectrum, an unranked player (zero stars) is deemed below average, not suited for Division I football, and destined for football mediocrity in the eyes of the recruiting pundits.

As you know, the Super Bowl is a matchup of the top two teams in the NFL. Given that college football serves as the unofficial minor league for the NFL, one would think Super Bowl rosters, Philadelphia and New England for Super Bowl LII, would be chock-full of former four- and five-star recruits as these players are performing at the highest level of football in the world.

If you made that assumption, you would be flat-out wrong.

Across both teams, there were 104 total rostered players for Super Bowl LII. Of those players, a staggering 69 percent were either zero, two, or three stars coming out of high school, with 29 percent of those players being unranked (zero stars). Twenty-nine percent! Clearly, the college-football-recruiting rankings severely missed on those prospects as they not only reached the pinnacle of the football world by playing in the NFL, but they played for one of the top two teams in the league. Thankfully for them and football fans around the globe, college coaches and NFL general managers were able to assess these twenty-nine percenters by looking out their front windshields as opposed to their rearview mirrors.

Since 2000, I have frequently reflected on Cheryl's promotion and am appreciative of our collective foresight to consider her potential as opposed to strictly looking at her past experiences. As a reflective leader, I have also called upon this memory when coaching others to help them look at a recruitment process from a different angle.

As Wayne Gretzky would tell you, it is significantly easier to see where the puck currently resides than to anticipate where it is going. Similarly, it is easier to assess a static resume to understand where a candidate currently resides and much more difficult to anticipate where they are going. However, and this is the critical part, the Great One skates to where the puck is going because that is where success lies.

What is good for the Great One should be good for you too.

CHAPTER 20

Avoid Triangles in Communication

*The single biggest problem in communication
is the illusion that it has taken place.*
—GEORGE BERNARD SHAW

THROUGHOUT MY HIGH school years, I was educated on the strength of the triangle. In tenth-grade World History, I learned the Egyptians were ahead of their time in how they used nature's strongest shape to build the pyramids. In Geometry, I learned a triangle is the simplest polygon, yet has uniquely intricate properties that lend to its strength, including the triangle inequality theorem. Of course, my physics teacher would find it remiss if I didn't include the lessons he taught regarding force and how when it is applied to the corners of a triangle, the load is distributed down each side with equal compression. The bottom line of these lessons is that we have forever been made aware of the strength and power of the triangle.

The reason I take us back to the bustling halls of our high schools is because the lessons of the triangle we were taught within those walls must be modified once we enter the professional workforce (unless you're an engineer, and then I suggest you keep those lessons near and dear). As a professional, you must retrain your brain to understand that when it comes to constructing effective communication and relationships, triangles are actually quite weak and should be avoided at all costs.

In both our personal and professional lives, we've learned to steer clear of passive-aggressive behavior. When people display such behavior, it creates an atmosphere of tension, mistrust, and miscommunication, all of which can lead to a toxic environment. From a communication standpoint, the poster child for passive-aggressive behavior is our old high school friend, the triangle.

Triangular communication occurs when two people fail to communicate directly and bring in a third party to vent; one person communicates with another about yet another. This sounds confusing and inefficient because it is—the third person is extraneous to the discussion.

Unfortunately, triangulation occurs in both personal and professional communications. For example, in a personal setting, you may have unfortunately said something upsetting to one of your friends, and they, in turn, go to someone else to complain about you rather than come to you directly. Or maybe you've seen it in a professional environment: your manager makes a decision with which you disagree. Rather than approach your manager to discuss that decision with them, you turn to a colleague to complain about that very decision knowing full well your colleague has zero ability to affect the outcome of the manager's decision.

Without fail, whenever triangulation occurs and is left unchecked, foul feelings are just around the bend. Even worse than hurt feelings is the fact that triangulation can severely damage the bedrock of all relationships—trust. Once distrust enters the equation, toxicity isn't far behind—all because someone triangulated the conversation and brought in a third party to "vent."

Triangulating someone into your own challenging situation by venting only temporarily relieves your anxiety. Oftentimes, people who feel helpless to change their own situation seek to transfer their frustration onto someone else by complaining about the person who has offended them. However, any assumed release of stress and anxiety is clearly temporary and carries the same effects of a drug—it will be short lived, and will most certainly require more the next time to get the same relief.

The good news is the solution to triangular communication is simple. The bad news is that triangular communications have been around since the building of the pyramids, and unfortunately, the pyramids will likely fall before triangular communications have been fully eradicated. Although humans are fallible, we can be trained, and through training, we can lessen the prevalence of this unfortunate form of communication.

Below are six simple actions you can take to ensure you don't get caught up in this unproductive form of communication. Furthermore, as a manager or leader, you can model this behavior with the people you lead or will lead.

1. **SET CLEAR EXPECTATIONS:** Establish clear expectations for communication within your relationships or team. Emphasize the importance of direct communication and discourage triangulation.

2. **ADDRESS ISSUES DIRECTLY:** When you have a concern or issue with someone, address it directly with that person. Avoid discussing the matter with a third party as your primary means of communication. If someone approaches you with a concern regarding another person, politely guide them back to the person who is at the root of that concern. When you personally take this approach, you will model this communication for others.

3. **ENCOURAGE OPEN DIALOGUE:** As a leader, you must foster an environment where open and honest communication is encouraged and celebrated. Make it clear that individuals should feel comfortable expressing their thoughts freely.

4. **CLARIFY MISUNDERSTANDINGS PROMPTLY:** If you become aware of misinformation or misunderstandings, address them promptly. There is an adage that states you should not let the sun set on your anger. In reality, you may not fully resolve a misunderstanding in a day, but you should at least try and clear the air as soon as possible.

5. SEEK MEDIATION IF NECESSARY: If a conflict arises and direct communication is challenging, consider involving a neutral third party as an informal mediator. Another leader or manager can help facilitate a constructive conversation and resolution between the parties.

6. ENCOURAGE FACE-TO-FACE COMMUNICATION: Whenever possible, opt for face-to-face communication. This allows for a more nuanced and direct exchange of thoughts and feelings, reducing the likelihood of miscommunication. Too often challenges are exacerbated over the phone or via email, where there is a lack of body language and the ability to read the room is diminished. Don't fan the flame by trying to be efficient with your communication.

When someone attempts to triangulate a conversation with you about someone else, you have three options: (1) you can join in; (2) you can offer to mediate; or (3) you can redirect them to the source of their challenge. Throughout my career, I have attempted to choose door number three and redirect the person back to the one single person who can truly resolve their frustrations—the person at the root of any frustration. I've not been perfect in utilizing this redirect, but I've seen it modeled for me countless times, and I'm hopeful I've modeled it for others.

I have experienced far too many examples of this unfortunate communication gaffe to include them within these pages. They all sound the same and they all end the same—when there is a lack of communication; negativity and toxicity will fill the void.

My goal in sharing this lesson learned is to highlight the challenges that exist within triangular communications, provide you with encouragement to model appropriate behaviors, and supply you with tools to eradicate them.

In case any of you have foggy memories of Geometry and have forgotten what the triangle inequality theorem is, allow me to refresh your memory. This theorem states that the length of any side of a triangle must always be less than the sum of the other two sides. While this theorem adds to the triangle's stability and rigidity in physics and mathematics, it highlights the weakness of a triangle in communication: the sum of the two primary sides will always be greater than the third leg.

Don't create, feed, or foster the third leg.

Sales

CHAPTER 21

Fall in Love with Their Problem, Not Your Solution

The art of conversation lies in listening.
—MALCOLM FORBES

HAVE YOU EVER encountered a "one-upper"—someone who seemingly has experienced every experience you've ever had, but always better? *Saturday Night Live* found enough humor in these types of people that they had an ongoing skit starring Kristin Wiig that comically portrayed this unfortunate personality trait.

As much humor as we might find in watching this unfold on the television screen on a Saturday night, this behavior in real life can clear a room quicker than tear gas. It isn't enjoyable to be around someone who acts in this manner because it is painfully evident the one-upper cares more about themselves than anyone else in the room.

The reason why this is so distasteful (and sometimes humorous) is that one of our primal human needs is to be heard. When this fundamental need is not met, it leads to frustration and disengagement. When it is met, it creates an environment where individuals thrive both emotionally and intellectually. Unfortunately, when a one-upper bursts into a room, there is only one person for whom this primal human need will be met—themselves.

The equivalent of this in a professional world is the salesperson who enters a meeting with a solution to every problem before the problems are even presented. The salesperson enjoys spending more time talking about their solution than any real attempt to understand the buyer's problem. Unfortunately, the professional world is full of sales one-uppers, and I have encountered my fair share of them throughout my career. These individuals show up to a meeting with a thirty-page PowerPoint deck and the meeting begins once they launch slide one and concludes once they advance to slide thirty—without any real desire shown for trying to better understand the buyer's current situation or problems.

Said differently, these unfortunate sales professionals have fallen in love with their solution and cannot wait to force it into whatever problem the buyer may have. Square peg? Round hole? Doesn't matter.

In these situations, the sales process has become more about the salesperson than the buyer—the sales one-upper simply wants to hear their own voice because they self-identified themselves to be an expert. Don't get me wrong. Being an expert is both appropriate and admirable in sales, but in order to build a trusting relationship and win the heart of the buyer, the salesperson cannot suck the oxygen out of a room. They must allow their buyer to breathe.

Too often, salespeople get caught up in the expert paradox—the more you think you know, the less you try to learn. Most every successful salesperson likes to consider themselves an expert in the very thing they are selling—whether it is a widget or a service. While this may be true and can ultimately be an arrow in a salesperson's quiver, they must initially enter a sales situation sincerely wanting to learn more about the prospect's current situation than trying to demonstrate their expertise. There is a time for the salesperson to flip the switch and share their expert knowledge, but only after they have gathered sufficient information from the buyer to be empathetic to the situation—and that only comes by asking questions and listening significantly more than speaking.

The most successful salespeople invest considerable time and energy to understand the buyer's current state, their current challenges, their history, and their desires. They ask open-ended questions with a sincere desire to learn more about the buyer. They are genuinely curious—they listen, they probe, and they restate. Their goal is to *fall in love with the buyer's problem*, and they work diligently to achieve it.

The above point is what separates good salespeople from great salespeople and is worth repeating—great salespeople work the sales process to fall in love with the buyer's problem, and they passionately seek it out.

One of the best examples of this sales approach came in working with a longtime friend, colleague, and, ultimately, competitor, Rob Haddad. Rob and I knew each other in college and then our families became friends over the years as our children grew up together. Professionally, Rob and I have been on both sides of the sales table, partnering together and competing against one another, and I have a great deal of respect for his ability to build relationships and listen to his clients.

This exemplary sales situation arose shortly after I had started MillsonJames in 2010 and we were partnering with his insurance agency. Rob asked us to join him in pursuing a whale of a prospect. Based on the size of the opportunity, he knew it would be a long sales cycle, and he had the right mindset from the get-go. Never once did Rob walk them through his thirty-page solutions-oriented PowerPoint. Instead, he worked to fall in love with their problems, and then he created unique solutions to address those problems. It is not an exaggeration to say he met with this prospect fifteen-plus times over several years, looking to learn more about their problems in each of those meetings.

Rob's empathetic approach allowed him to build a genuine relationship with the prospect. He never once one-upped them. Although it took several years to land this career-defining client, he ultimately did, and I firmly believe it was because of his selfless approach.

I often reflect on this sales process and have used it to coach others to approach the sales process in a buyer-centric manner. In doing so, a salesperson accomplishes several things:

1. They put the focus on the buyer, not themselves;

2. They invert the motivation of the sale by seeking to help the buyer versus seeking to help themselves (and trust me: this inversion is quite evident to the buyer); and

3. They train their brain to listen more than they speak. God gave us two ears and one mouth and we should use them in direct proportion.

From Year 1 to Year 34 of my career, when I found myself rubbing elbows with an exceptional sales professional, I very intentionally tuned in to their frequency of excellence. I learned a great deal by watching how each of these professionals conducted their meetings, how they handled objections, and how they built relationships through genuine curiosity about the buyer. However, above all, the single greatest and most attractive trait found in each of the exceptional sales professionals with whom I've worked: they listened, and they worked to fall in love with the buyer's problem.

At the end of the day, sales is but a microcosm of everyday society. What a buyer expects and appreciates in a sales process is no different than what a person expects and appreciates in their everyday lives—to be around people who listen and appreciate what they have to say. They want to be heard and not one-upped. They want the problems they share to be truly understood and not dismissed with a preset soliloquy of solutions.

My encouragement for any salesperson is to fall in love with your buyer's problem. Listen. Probe. Restate. Have the sales process be more about the buyer than you.

Don't be a one-upper.

Be more like Rob.

CHAPTER 22

Build a Diverse, Genuine, and Equally Yoked Network

The currency of real networking is not greed but generosity.
—KEITH FERRAZZI

L
ONG BEFORE A guy named Zuckerberg ever attended Harvard, I was encouraged to develop a strong network. In the early 1990s, I wasn't entirely sure what the term meant or how it could benefit me; however, I was encouraged to meet a wide array of individuals, collaborate with diverse groups, and seek out a variety of experiences. Above all, and this one came directly from my mother at a young age, I was encouraged to be as genuine as possible when developing relationships.

Fast-forward thirty-plus years, and we have been rewired to a new definition of the word *network* that consists of connections, subscribers, followers, and even "friends." Most recently, we have witnessed the rise of the social media influencer and the drive to obtain (or now purchase) the verified, yet elusive, blue checkmark. To be perfectly clear, I am not knocking the evolution of today's social networks as I utilize and appreciate several platforms. It is a natural occurrence for the world to adapt and evolve—and it has. That said, in my opinion, the traditional definition and value of a strong, diverse, and *genuine* professional network has stood the test of time and will continue well into the future, despite the ubiquity of social media.

Throughout my career, I have been fortunate to work with several outstanding employers across several geographies and within several

107

related industries, all of which created a good bit of breadth and diversity within my network. In each of these situations, with my mother's encouragement ringing in my ears, I worked to build genuine and meaningful relationships with my coworkers, clients, and business partners. Not only did these experiences help build my Reflection Collection, but also they helped me assist others, further my career, further the careers of others, and build businesses. When I launched MillsonJames in 2010, I very intentionally called upon my network and asked them for referrals to help create initial sales opportunities. When my oldest son, Sam, launched his consulting firm ten years later, the power of our collective networks was once again on full display as he successfully launched and grew the Millson Group.

As powerful a broad and diverse network can appear to be, the real value lies in the depth and genuineness of the relationships that create it. Had my network relationships been insincere and shallow when I called upon it to launch MillsonJames, my request for referrals would have been met with the painful sound of crickets. Because the depth of the relationships within my network were genuine and battle tested, I received actionable referrals from people who knew I would do the very same for them.

It has been my experience that one of the quickest ways to determine the genuineness of a professional relationship is to assess whether it is mutually beneficial. If a network relationship is one-sided and unequally yoked, it will never produce the results you hope to achieve. Over the years, I have developed an allergic reaction to and an acute distaste for BS. When I sense the genuineness of a connection is weak or the potential for a relationship is entirely one-sided, I focus my attention elsewhere. Life is simply too short to be in unequally yoked relationships.

In today's digital world, it is too easy to be attracted to volume—number of subscribers, followers, or connections. Those look good on the surface, but if you ever intend to utilize the network you have built, you must ensure the relationships are equally yoked. Building a network that is a mile wide, yet an inch deep is akin to building a house on sand—it lacks the proper foundation and likely won't stand the test of time or deliver the value you seek. However, when you build a home (or a network) on a solid foundation, it is built to withstand the ages and deliver timeless value.

I was reminded of this truism when I recently came across a LinkedIn post from a former colleague—Trish Kendall (née Trout). Trish and I had worked together on the Sageo business in the early 2000s, and we quickly became friends. Trish was an exceptional salesperson whose optimism and love for life was undeniable and contagious. We enjoyed working with one another, but lost touch once I left Hewitt in 2006. Fast-forward sixteen years, and I came across a LinkedIn video Trish had posted the evening before in which she was highlighting her consulting company and her growing speaking business. I reached out the next morning to catch up and learn more about her new endeavor.

Reconnecting with long-lost friends on social media is nothing new, I freely admit. However, what made this reconnection unique is what happened upon reconnecting. Since that initial reconnection, I hired Trish to provide a keynote address for the business I led at the time, and she returned the favor by helping me refine my thinking for this book. That, my friends, is the true definition of a mutually beneficial, equally yoked, and genuine network relationship.

The ability for Trish and me to quickly reconnect is because we had laid a foundation of genuine respect for one another in the early 2000s, which made it easy to begin working together again and mutually benefiting one another—as if no time had passed at all.

In the end, networking isn't about reaching out to or collecting as many people as possible. It's about connecting with people from whom you can learn—and who might learn from you—regardless of whether there is a platform behind it.

Networking today is no different than it was before Mr. Zuckerberg arrived. Relationships must be genuine and mutually beneficial, just as my mother suggested so many years ago.

Blue checkmark be damned.

CHAPTER 23

There Is a Difference between Listening and Waiting Your Turn to Speak

I remind myself every morning: Nothing I
say this day will teach me anything. So if I'm
going to learn, I must do it by listening.

—LARRY KING

WHEN I FOUNDED MillsonJames in 2010, I was fortunate to have worked alongside and for some of the greatest minds in the consulting industry, particularly at Hewitt Associates. I was determined to leverage all the experiences stored in my Collection to create a firm that was second to none in terms of knowledge, experience, objectivity, client-relationship building, and, most importantly, listening skills.

The senior consultants at Hewitt engaged with Fortune 500 executives as if they were interacting with family and friends. Their consulting appeared effortless and I worked to ensure my observation skills were on high alert every time I was fortunate enough to ride shotgun on one of their client or prospect calls. Client meetings at Hewitt were always conversational; the discussions flowed naturally and never felt scripted or rote. As such, Hewitt's clients felt respected and appreciated being heard.

One of my opportunities to ride shotgun stands out and provided me with one of the greatest reflections of my career. We were called to meet with a Fortune 50 client that was contemplating hiring Hewitt for a new service—a service that, as of 1998, had never before been offered or executed by our organization or, frankly, any organization within our industry. The client's request was for us to build a 24-7 contact center for their global HR operation, and we were assessing the opportunity and identifying the best path forward. I was, by far, the most junior consultant involved in the project as I was sitting alongside Brian Caffarelli and Mike Wright, both of whom were senior partners/owners at Hewitt, and both of whom were known to be among the best consultants within our organization.

I prepared for the meeting by researching the client's request as best I could, learning as much as possible about the technology they were asking us to support, and about 24-7 global contact centers. When I sat down with Brian and Mike to review my carefully prepared notes and information, they reframed the meeting for me and very politely encouraged me to set my prepared notes/questions aside.

They informed me we had one simple goal for this initial meeting—to listen.

Given the uniqueness of the client's request, we could not present ourselves as any form of an expert in this arena. We hoped Hewitt could support their request, but there was no way for us to enter that meeting room with a proposed solution in mind. Rather than guess and present, we focused all of our energies on preparing ourselves to listen, learn, and fall in love with their problem.

As recommended, I entered the meeting with my notes tucked away in my briefcase and my mind focused on actively listening to our client. However, what really occurred is that I became a pupil in a consulting master class. I witnessed both Mike and Brian carefully dissect the client's request by asking open-ended questions, asking follow-up questions, clarifying answers, restating comments, reframing requests, and truly seeking to understand. There was no script. There were no preconceived ideas or biases, only a sincere desire to listen and understand.

Although I cannot recall for certain where I first heard the phrase "there is a difference between listening and waiting your turn to speak," it was on full display in Tampa, Florida, in 1998. Never once did I feel as though Mike or Brian were waiting their turn to speak, ready to pounce with a preset question. Rather, their engagement was sincere, and they were intently listening and learning.

Not only did we achieve our objective of gathering information, but Mike and Brian's empathetic approach put the customer at ease. More importantly, the customer felt heard and appreciated.

Empathy is at the root of building effective relationships, whether personal or professional. We cannot build an effective relationship without first understanding the other person's experience by imagining ourselves in their situation. The foolproof way to understand someone else's perspective is to talk less and listen more.

Had Brian and Mike allowed me to enter the meeting with my preconfigured questions to ask or topics to cover, I would have been bound to that piece of paper and would have constantly been waiting my turn to speak and not truly listening. I was appreciative of that counsel in 1998 as well as the countless years that followed.

Roll forward twelve years and now I am launching MillsonJames and working to build our firm's consulting tools and resources from scratch. One of the primary consulting services we intended to provide our customers was an upfront discovery meeting, during which we would assess the current state, understand the client's challenges, and begin to develop a course of action. I had a fleeting thought that maybe I should create a list of questions we could use to guide our consultants through an initial client meeting. I say a fleeting thought, because I was quickly transported back to that 1998 meeting, and I heard Brian and Mike's voice remind me that the goal of an initial meeting should be to listen. I remembered how effortlessly Mike and Brian maneuvered the meeting by not following a script or list of questions and how comfortable it made the customer feel because we were sincerely listening to them versus waiting our turn to speak.

As a result of this reflection, we never created a list of questions to be used during our discovery meetings at MillsonJames. Listening became a key tenant of our firm and was the basis for how we consulted with our customers. Creating a script of questions would be brought up most every time a new consultant would join MillsonJames as they believed it would simplify and streamline our initial consultations. I recall many conversations with Margaret Godwin, a senior consultant with MillsonJames, where she would ask if she could develop her own set of discovery questions. I would politely listen to the request and then share with her the simple lesson I was taught by Mike Wright and Brian Caffarelli—the goal of a discovery meeting is to listen.

To be clear, not having a preset list of questions doesn't mean you don't have to prepare for a client or sales meeting, nor does it mean you shouldn't create an agenda. Preparation and setting expectations (via agendas) are critical to the success of any endeavor. However, your preparation should be focused on creating a foundation upon which you can build your knowledge of the customer, their background, and what you've learned to date.

I would encourage any consultant, salesperson, or anyone managing a client relationship to resist the temptation to script presentations for initial/Discovery Meetings. You should prepare for the meeting, of course. But don't get caught up in trying to perfect your line of questions or creating a multipage PowerPoint to share your point of view. By not following a specific line of questions, it will create freedom for you to truly listen and assess the need and opportunity.

Be creative. Be curious. Seek to understand.

Active listening worked for us in 1998 as we were awarded the Fortune 50 client's business, likely because we genuinely sought to understand their problem and weren't wed to any preconceived solution.

At the end of the day, you want your client to feel as though they were heard.

If you find yourself waiting for your turn to speak, you'll most certainly miss on achieving that goal.

CHAPTER 24

Sales Is a Dialogue, Not a Monologue

Dialogue is a process of genuine interaction through which human beings listen to each other deeply enough to be changed by what they learn.
—HAROLD SAUNDERS

WHILE THIS MAY sound strange coming from someone writing a book, I consider myself a moderate reader. If a spectrum existed to measure the passion of a reader, with reluctant at one end and voracious at the other, I would find myself squarely in the middle. While I have always enjoyed a good book and how it can move and shape my emotions and thinking, I have unfortunately struggled to find the time to move myself further to the right of this spectrum. With the positions I've held, the fitness activities I've enjoyed, and the family I've helped raise, most of my tiring days would end early in an effort to get a good night's sleep so I could restart the engine bright and early the next day.

The three primary exceptions to this were vacations, when I came across a topic about which I was currently passionate, or when I launched a Wisdom Quest. In these situations, I would move to the right of the spectrum and could devour a good book—oftentimes marking it up with a pen or highlighter for downstream recall/reference.

Such was the case in 2022 when my oldest son, Sam, and I were considering opening an Italian Ice franchise in his hometown of

Memphis, Tennessee. Sam had acquired Jeremiah's Italian Ice as a client of his industrial engineering consulting firm the year before and had been helping them with their supply chain, sales forecasting, and overall logistics. We were also quite familiar with the brand (and frequent customers) as it was founded in Winter Park, Florida, the town in which we raised our family. We knew the founder, many of the initial investors, and now Sam was becoming familiar with the inner workings of this growing business. It seemed like a great business in which to invest, and Kristin and I were excited to work with Sam to build a business together, so we jumped at the opportunity.

Although neither Sam nor I had any direct experience in running a restaurant, I had been exposed to launching and growing a food service business through a MillsonJames consulting relationship I'd had with 4 Rivers Smokehouse in the early 2010s. The owner of that business is a good friend and mentor, John Rivers. During my time consulting with John and his team, we grew 4 Rivers from three to fifteen restaurants throughout Florida. Yet even with that exceptional experience, I still felt as though I needed more information on operating a restaurant and developing a brand with unparalleled hospitality. With my father-in-law's voice in my head, I launched another Wisdom Quest, reached out to friends/colleagues in the hospitality industry, and searched for published authors who had experiences I wished to gain.

Following the recommendation of several people, I purchased a book written by Will Guidara entitled *Unreasonable Hospitality.* For those unfamiliar with this book, I'll provide you with a brief synopsis, but I highly recommend you read it as the lessons shared go well beyond hospitality and the restaurant industry and can and should be applied to any business venture. The book is a memoir, of sorts, and within it, Will shares the details of his journey from being the son of a restaurateur to his ascension to running the top restaurant in the world. Not *one of* the top restaurants, but *the number one restaurant in the world*—Eleven Madison Park (EMP) in New York City.

What is unique about Will's story is that his rise to the top was different than most everyone else in his industry. He worked relentlessly on the service side of the business while his business partner focused on the unique aspects and quality of the food. His goal was to differentiate the *experience* of the guest in ways that went beyond the norm, what he calls the remarkable power of giving people more than they expect.

As informative and powerful his hospitality messages were to both Sam and me as it related to our new Italian Ice venture, it was the broader business lessons I took from the book that left me wanting more. His lessons and approaches provided me with unique insights into leadership, mentorship, management, customer service, and, as you may have guessed based on the title of this chapter, sales.

Within the book, Will shares a quote from one of his mentors, Danny Meyer, of Gramercy Tavern and Shake Shack fame. Danny believes "hospitality is a dialogue, not a monologue,"[5] and his protégé took that not only to heart but also to the extreme. In the book, Will shares how he worked diligently with the servers at EMP to engage customers in a true dialogue about their menu—moving on from the traditional one-directional monologue. He didn't just want his servers to share the details of the menu and how excellent the prepared dishes were, he wanted to gather input from the guest as to what they liked, what they didn't like, and what they were hoping to experience. Will wanted the customer to be a cast member of the EMP experience, not just a member of the audience.

I was moved by this comparison of a dialogue versus monologue and how it expands beyond the walls of EMP and into every office building in America in which a sales process occurs. Too often, sales professionals engage in what they believe to be an all-important monologue about their product or service. They have perfected their speech. They know every value proposition by heart. They have researched every potential objection and, in their eyes, have built immaculate responses to those anticipated barriers. The problem with this sales approach is that it is entirely one-sided, and the person to whom the product or service is being sold has not been able to truly share what they like, what they don't like, and what they are hoping to experience.

This outcome is exactly the experience Will was trying to avoid when he built EMP into the number one restaurant in the world. He didn't want a one-sided conversation with a guest, as that had been the norm with every fine dining restaurant ever rated by Michelin. From the Bib Gourmand to the three-star restaurants Michelin rates, the intense focus of those restaurants had been historically focused on the quality and uniqueness of the food, treating the guest interaction as important but secondary. At those restaurants, the servers were schooled in the science of the meal, in its unique preparation, and had a clear understanding that zero substitutions were allowed because of how precisely the chef had created a particular dish. If a guest at one of these high-end restaurants disliked olives (which are nasty, by the way), the answer would be stated as kindly as possible, "too bad," because the chef felt it was critical to the dish. Will did not want any version of "too bad" to be a part of the dialogue at EMP—and it wasn't.

What Will recognized is that while the food needed to be of the highest quality, the customer needed to be on equal footing and fully engaged in the ordering experience. There needed to be an *exchange of information*. If the customer disliked a particular ingredient, Will wanted to know that information so he and his partner, Daniel, would create a dish that avoided the dreaded item. Will understood, "the most profound moments come through specific and thoughtful gestures that demonstrate that the restaurant cares enough to listen to what you say and then to do something with what they've heard."[6]

Dialogue > Monologue.

I would encourage all sales professionals to recall this story the next time you're leading a sales process. Are you truly engaging with the customer? Do you honestly understand their needs and their wants? Do you know if they have a distaste for olives or whatever might be the equivalent of olives in your sales pitch?

The buyer wants to be a cast member, not just an audience member. They want to be part of a genuine dialogue.

Like Will Guidara, buyers understand and appreciate "the most profound moments come through specific and thoughtful gestures that demonstrate that [your business] cares enough to listen to what [the buyer] says and then [the salesperson] does something with what [you've heard]."

The goal of every salesperson should be to do something that stirs a buyer's emotion to a profound level. That is how you take your business to number one—in the world!

Hold the olives, please.

CHAPTER 25

Be a Guide, Not a Porter

The real voyage of discovery consists not in seeking
new landscapes, but in having new eyes.
—MARCEL PROUST

T RAVELING TO A foreign country can be intimidating. For
that matter, traveling to a domestic destination for the first time
can be equally as intimidating. You don't know the area, you're
not sure of the cultural dos and don'ts, and you're certainly not sure
which attractions to frequent or avoid. Of course, you always have
the internet to rely upon, and sites like Tripadvisor can be helpful.
However, while those resources are valuable, because you're trading a
day or week of your life for the trip (not to mention your hard-earned
money), you want to ensure your time at the destination meets your
expectations and creates a memorable experience.

For any larger vacation our family has taken, we have found it
is helpful to use a local guide in some way, shape, or form. These
guides are experts in the region, have lived in the community for
some time, and have already experienced most everything that we
are hoping to experience. Furthermore, the best guides have a sincere appreciation for their region and they have an innate desire to
share that with others.

My most memorable experience with a guide came on a business
trip I took to India in January 2005. The Your Spending Account
(YSA) business I was leading at that time was heavily leveraging a

team out of Gurgaon, India, and we had not yet had the opportunity to meet the team.

As noted at the onset of this chapter, traveling to a foreign country can be intimidating. Traveling nineteen hours to a country about which I knew very little was alarming and a good bit overwhelming. I tried to learn as much as I could about the culture, received five different vaccinations, and accepted a host of travel warnings from the Orlando Health Travel Center. Despite feeling anxious about the trip, I believed I had adequately prepared myself.

That feeling of preparedness lasted all of two minutes upon our arrival in New Delhi. I was in sensory overload, with four of my five senses being pushed to their absolute limits when we visited a local market. *Sight:* there were tens of thousands of people jammed into the compact market, with limited room to walk anywhere. To give you a sense for the chaos, picture yourself at halftime of your favorite college football stadium fighting to locate the concession stand; yet halftime never ends. *Sound:* given the color of our skin, we stood out at the market. All eyes were trained on us with hundreds of peddlers attracted to us like moths to a flame, barking in our ears, "Mister, mister, please buy. One hundred rupees, pleeeeeasssse!" *Touch:* as we were being sold the varied local Indian products, the locals were tugging on our clothes and grabbing our arms to gain our attention. *Smell:* the locals burn cow dung cakes for fuel and the earthy aroma hovers heavily in the air.

Each of these unique experiences surpassed any forewarning I received from Tripadvisor or the travel nurses. I quickly realized that we had ventured well beyond the familiar.

The following day was a Sunday, and we knew this was our only opportunity to visit the Taj Mahal, India's entry into the Seven Wonders of the World. I was determined not to miss seeing the Taj; yet I was aware that reaching the town of Agra meant enduring a four-hour car journey, mostly on back roads, some of which were unpaved, winding through small villages, and navigating around water buffalo, cows, and chickens leisurely wandering down the center of many of these roads.

We recognized our travel to the Taj Mahal would require the use of a porter (local driver) to ensure a safe arrival and a guide (local expert) to enhance our visit. While both were critical for our visit to the Taj, it was the hiring of our local guide, Sunil, that created long-lasting and powerful memories.

Sunil was a college-educated local from Agra who was working to save up enough money for a sizable dowry for his younger sister "to ensure she marries well." While this concept was foreign to us, he shared the unique history behind this tradition, and we were appreciative of the lesson and gained unique insights into Indian culture. Before we began our tour of the Taj, Sunil asked us a host of questions to better understand our backgrounds and to learn what we hoped to gain from exploring his hometown and experiencing the grandeur of India's iconic monument. This unexpected, yet appreciated, step in his process made for a very special experience.

As we approached the Taj Mahal, he described, in intricate detail, the marble works and in-lain semiprecious stones that were used to build the temple as well as its history. He also highlighted for us the strikingly unique aspect of the Taj Mahal—the picture-perfect symmetry of the temple, down to the smallest millimeter. I knew nothing of these things prior to our arrival, so I was deeply appreciative of Sunil and his knowledge of the Taj Mahal and the surrounding area.

Following our visit to the Taj, Sunil took us on remarkable tours of a local marble shop, carpet factory, and Agra Fort—all areas I would have missed or skipped had we tried to visit the Taj Mahal on our own or simply relied on impersonal internet searches. Sunil was the quintessential professional, a real expert in Indian culture and an exceptional storyteller of the beauty that is the final resting place of Mumtaz Majal. I could not imagine our visit without him; he undeniably enhanced our experience.

I share this story because of the uncanny parallel that exists between an effective guide and an effective salesperson. I have repeatedly reflected on the excellence of Sunil as our guide and I've tried to coach sales professionals to perform in a similar manner.

As a salesperson, you have the unique ability to be a professional version of Sunil for your clients. You have the expertise, you know how the process works, you have conducted a similar sales process hundreds of times, and you know the potential shortcomings. You, and you alone, can guide your prospective customer to help reduce the stress and intimidation of a sales process. In being an effective guide for your clients, you can undeniably enhance your customer's experience.

Much like the intimidation I felt on my visit to India, a buyer can feel the same pressures when they engage in a sales process. This is foreign territory for a buyer in that they may only perform this process a few times in a career. The perceived pressure can be significant and the buyer can quickly become overwhelmed. In some extreme situations and depending on the size of the deal, the decisions they have been tasked to make can be career making or breaking.

A good friend and mentor of mine, Brian Caffarelli, once noted, "If you think selling is hard, buying is harder." There is such truth in those words and yet, oftentimes as salespeople, we become myopic and feel nothing is more difficult than closing a deal. Understanding that buying is equally as hard, if not harder than selling, will help you be an empathetic guide for your customer.

Brian was one of the first people I knew to use the metaphor of guides and porters in a sales process. Both he and Trish Kendall, an exceptional consultant and coach in her own right, continually use this metaphor to effectively coach business development professionals. In Trish's case, we hired her to deliver this very message to our HUB teams and to encourage them to create, as she calls it, "enduring success" with clients.

Porters play a vital role in transporting either us or our luggage from point A to point B. While our driver safely escorted us to the

Taj Mahal, it was Sunil who emerged as the true hero of our Taj experience. As our guide, he enriched our adventure by sharing his extensive local knowledge and ensuring we enjoyed every moment to the fullest.

In a sales process, your clients must move from point A to point B, and most any salesperson will serve as a porter to help them do so. However, if your desire is to build relationships with enduring success that help you achieve your short- and long-term goals, you must step into the role of a trusted guide.

Your customers will be incredibly appreciative when you do, just as we were with Sunil.

Leadership

CHAPTER 26

Be a Laughing Leader

There is little success where there is little laughter.
—ANDREW CARNEGIE

I WAS DROPPED INTO a situation at Hewitt Associates in 1990, where I was surrounded by a group of leaders and associates who worked hard and played equally as hard—a great environment in which to first experience professional living. The leaders in the Hewitt Atlanta office set this tone for me. We took the responsibility of serving our customers very seriously and were committed to the task at hand. We worked exceptionally hard—often sixty to eighty hours/week; however, when the time was right, we would enjoy ourselves, poke fun at one another, and laugh often. No one was immune. From the senior leaders in our office to the new kid on the block, the expectation was clear—be a serious person, but don't take yourself too seriously. Whether it was a fiscal-year kickoff skit or the typical April Fools' high jinks, it made the occasional eighty-hour workweeks much more tolerable.

When I transferred to the Hewitt New Jersey office in 1993, I recall hoping there would be a similar focus on working hard and playing hard, and I was certainly not disappointed. Upon arrival in New Jersey, I remember quickly meeting folks like Mark Arian, Ron Lloyd, and Bernie Stiroh and feeling a sense of relief that this mantra of not taking ourselves too seriously was a firmwide focus. I shared a lot of laughs with these leaders, and they helped further the belief that in order for someone to be willing to put in the extra effort a customer may demand, you needed to look forward to coming to work each day—both for the work and for the laughter. Humor is important in the workplace because it reminds us of our humanness. When no one feels comfortable to be themselves, no one will feel comfortable to be creative or take risks.

As a leader, I have found it helpful to set the work bar high and yet raise the bar to a similar level for having fun in the office. I've come to realize that a laughing leader is authentic. No one can be serious all the time, and, candidly, no one wants to work for that leader.

Laughter is also healthy for the workplace and your teammates. Countless studies demonstrate that a common denominator in high-performing teams is laughter. Laughter has a binding effect and can bring a team together, in good times and in bad. When we laugh, we release a cocktail of hormones as well as create physical changes in our bodies. According to one study by the Mayo Clinic, laughter stimulates your organs by enhancing the intake of oxygen rich air while also stimulating your heart, lungs, and muscles.[7] Additionally, laughter increases the endorphins that are released by your brain and provides a shot of dopamine, the same release that occurs while having sex.

Dopamine triggers the brain's reward pathway, intensifying your desire for these activities. As a leader, when you establish a culture of being serious but not taking ourselves too seriously, you create an environment in which people want to take part, are more productive, and simply look forward to coming to work every day. Be sure to laugh with your teammates, even when things aren't going exactly according to plan, because laughter also lowers cortisol, the primary stress hormone.

These benefits can be helpful in all parts of business, including, and most notably in, sales and client management. The same cocktail of hormones noted above can be triggered and released in a sales conversation, when used appropriately. Sharing a laugh with a prospective customer helps build rapport and establishes a connection that makes the interaction more comfortable and authentic for the buyer. It can also be used to break the tension that may exist when a buyer is less than excited to meet with a salesperson. Let's be honest: people are more likely to buy from individuals they like and with whom they feel comfortable. A well-placed joke or a good sense of humor can enhance the salesperson's likability, thereby increasing the chances of a successful interaction and, ideally, a successful sale.

I will categorically deny this when and if he reads it, but I've seen a good friend of mine, Alex Place, use this arrow in his quiver more effectively than most. Alex has a way to disarm a prospect with humor. He's able to make a connection that is genuine and engaging. His use of dad jokes is at an Olympic level, but it works as he is consistently one of the highest-performing salespeople within his organization. I attribute much of his success to his ability to connect with his clients and prospects through humor.

As with anything, there needs to be guardrails for humor in the workplace and you, as a leader, must establish those guardrails as well as set the boundaries that should not be crossed. Don't ever become a leader who teases staff members or tells off-color jokes. Not only is this inappropriate and distasteful, but also you set the model for others to follow. Don't be a leader that tolerates these behaviors.

However, when you keep the humor within the standard bounds of decency, laughter is a great way to establish culture and reward people for going above and beyond. Work can be stressful, but when you inject laughter, you'll begin to watch the cortisol levels drop and success levels rise.

Luckily for me, I was able to learn and experience this lesson rather early in my career, and it was reinforced at each port along the way.

John Maxwell famously once said, "We take our mission seriously, but not ourselves."

May the same be true for all of you who are called to lead.

CHAPTER 27

We Organizations > Me Organizations

Individually, we are one drop. Together, we are an ocean.
—RYUNOSUKE SATORO

W HEN I JOINED Hewitt Associates in 1990, the firm was on the cusp of celebrating its fiftieth anniversary, and there were a host of planned activities, gifts, and nostalgia events aimed at documenting our rich history and celebrating everything that made Hewitt such a unique place to work. Hewitt had built a strong reputation for having a distinct culture that was heavily sought after by both potential employees and clients. It was an exceptional place to work, as recognized and defined by their inclusion in a 1984 book entitled *The 100 Best Companies to Work For in America.*

Those were the golden years of Hewitt—tightly held partnership, free food for all associates,* and a laser-like focus on creating

---

* The free food reference above is worthy of further explanation and detail. From roughly 1941 to 2004, Hewitt Associates offered a unique employee benefit—free food and drink for all associates. To be fair, Hewitt was an employee benefit consulting company, and so we were often on the cutting edge of what we offered our own associates, but the benefit was truly remarkable and consisted of breakfast, lunch, drinks, and snacks. Depending on the office to which you were assigned, afternoon snacks consisted of cookie carts or Ben & Jerry's bars. My waistline in those early years only wished I was kidding with the last part.

consulting excellence in every aspect of our client relationships. At the root of all Hewitt's historical success was an unwavering belief that it was clearly a *we* organization—an organization that valued teamwork, collaboration, and a suppression of self-promotion.

This concept of *we > me* was foundational for the organization and permeated all aspects of the business and culture. From the client letters we wrote to the lack of titles on our business cards, the focus was always on the organization and not the individual.

As a case in point and to ensure consistency across the firm, there was a very specific way in which we were to format the letters used to communicate with our clients. In the early 1990s, 100 percent of all client communication was facilitated via a typewritten or word-processed letter. Whether we were summarizing a client meeting, following up on an opportunity, documenting the results of our research, or working to open an opportunity, it was communicated with a letter to be sent via US Mail or FedEx (née Federal Express).

One of the more consistently applied Hewitt rules was that the words *I* or *me* were to *never* be used within a client correspondence. Never. Ever. Everything was *we*. It didn't matter if you were documenting a meeting in which you were the only Hewitt Associate present—your summary letter would reference how much *we* appreciated meeting with the client, how *we* would be getting back with them on follow-up items, and the actions *we* would be taking. Furthermore, the salutation of every Hewitt Associates letter would read:

Sincerely,

HEWITT ASSOCIATES
Scott A. Millson

The words Hewitt Associates always preceded the consultant's name. Why? Because when we were communicating with a client, we were always representing and communicating as the broader organization, not the individual.

We always worked within a team environment, and the team was always held above the individual. Put it this way: if Hewitt Associates were a football team, I can assure you there would be no names on the back of our jerseys. It was all about the Hewitt Associates name on the front of the jersey. Everything was about the team or, as we lovingly referred to it, the firm.

Again, this mentality and culture extended throughout the organization, not just client correspondence. It was a *we* culture through and through. The CEO's office was the same size as mine. His business card was identical to mine, minus the obvious name difference, and included no title. The result of this was a pure and sincere acknowledgment that *we* is greater than *me*.

Our associates felt and appreciated it, which meant our clients felt and appreciated it. Our clients knew, when they hired Hewitt, they were getting the power of an entire team, not just an individual consultant. This unique and selfless culture is a primary reason Hewitt had decades of double-digit growth and scores of satisfied clients.

The benefits of working within a *we*-oriented organization are many and obvious. When everyone is working together for a common goal, the wheels of progress tend to turn more easily, and results tend to be longer-lasting and more enjoyable to obtain. *We* organizations tend to value collaboration and celebrate team victories versus individual successes. Professional sport teams are the epitome of *we* organizations and every owner, GM, and coach works feverishly to build *we* organizations because they understand the power of *we* always exceeds the power of *me*. This is why most every professional athlete would rather win a Super Bowl, World Series, or NBA Championship as opposed to winning an individual MVP award—the power of *we* over *me*.

As a reflective leader, this lesson has served me well throughout my career, as both a leader and an employee, and I would encourage you to add it to your own Reflection Collection as well. Seek out *we* organizations. Build *we* organizations. Foster an environment that celebrates *we* over *me*. The results are powerful, I can assure you.

The power of the team always exceeds the power of the individual and building a culture that recognizes, appreciates, and values this will always win.

The many lessons taught to me by the culture of Hewitt were certainly long lasting, but the power of *we > me* was among the strongest lessons of all.

CHAPTER 28

Take More Blame; Accept Less Credit

Leadership is a combination of strategy and character.
If you must be without one, be without the strategy.
—US GENERAL H. NORMAN SCHWARZKOPF

THERE ARE A handful of books that are permanently etched within my Reflection Collection—books that were inspiring and instrumental in developing and shaping my leadership philosophies, management strategies, and sales perspectives. While reading each of these books, I was able to tune in to the frequency of excellence of the author and take one, two, ten, or twenty lessons from each and gratefully apply them to my Collection. I've included a list of these books in the appendix in hopes that you may be encouraged to pick one of them up and have it inspire you in the same way it did me.

One of these books is *Good to Great*, written by Jim Collins and published in 2001. This book quickly became a bestseller and was a "must-read" for any executive leading a business at the turn of the century. Hewitt's leadership fell in line as we were all encouraged to read the book and it was discussed frequently at various Hewitt leadership events. I have read *Good to Great* several times and each time I read it, I'm introduced to a new way of thinking I'd not seen previously. However, the one lesson that remains constant no matter how many times I read it is the concept of a Level 5 Leader.

The unique aspect of *Good to Great* is that it is primarily data and research-driven. Jim Collins and his research team identified a set of companies that significantly outperformed (at least three times) the capital markets over a fifteen-year period, and they analyzed those companies' characteristics to help identify common threads. One of the key traits of organizations that made the leap from being merely good to achieving sustained greatness was that they all were led by a Level 5 Leader.

A Level 5 Leader is characterized by having a combination of personal humility and professional will. More specifically as it relates to humility, a Level 5 Leader "looks out the **window** to apportion credit to factors outside of themselves when things go well. At the same time, they look in the **mirror** to apportion responsibility when things go poorly."[8] This particular lesson immediately struck a chord with me, and I've worked diligently to leverage and reflect this "window/ mirror" component of a Level 5 Leader ever since.

I have witnessed countless situations in my career that speak to the humility of a leader and their willingness to pass along the credit to the teams they lead. Each of those situations have helped positively shape my approach to leadership. However, I have also witnessed the unfortunate passing of blame from a leader and it has similarly shaped me into knowing what not to do when things don't go as planned.

It is often said character is revealed when pressure is applied. As it relates to leadership, the true essence of a leader is uncovered in both challenging and celebratory times. I have found there is a direct correlation in the strength of a leader and the amount of blame a leader is willing to accept when the chips are down. Conversely, the amount of credit a leader is willing to accept when things are going well and the strength of that same leader are inversely correlated. As a leader, it is incumbent upon you to take more of the blame (mirror) and accept less of the credit (window).

I've witnessed two clear examples of leadership in trying times that stand out for me—one serves as a vivid memory of how not to lead and the other as an example of leadership at its finest.

The unfortunate example happened within a business unit to which I was loosely connected. This business unit was charged with servicing an exceptionally challenging and demanding client—a client that had a history of being unreasonable and, at times, unprofessional. There were constant fires with this client, and the relationship was always on the rocks. There came a time when the client noise hit a decibel level that attracted the attention of firm leadership at the highest levels. The leader of this business unit to which the client was assigned was appropriately asked to step in to help right the ship, which they did. However, when the firm's leadership asked for a summary of what the issues were and how things got back on track, this particular leader accepted far too much credit for the resolution and not nearly enough blame for the initial challenges. The outcome was unfortunate on many levels—the leader was too focused on self-promotion at the cost of blaming others on the team and, in doing so, lost the long-term respect of those the leader led.

On the flip side, the positive example of Level 5 Leadership is connected to one of the greatest leaders of my generation—General Colin Powell.

About the same time that Jim Collins's book was taking the business world by storm, there was growing unrest in the Middle East, specifically in Iraq. At the time, General Colin Powell was serving as secretary of state for the Bush administration, and his star couldn't have been positioned much higher. He was very well regarded throughout the world and had previously been encouraged to run for president in 1996, although he opted against it.

Despite his many achievements and powerful goodwill, General Powell's legacy could have forever been tarnished following his infamous 2003 speech to the UN in which he convinced the world that Iraq was producing weapons of mass destruction (WMD). Because of this, he argued, the United States would be justified in going to war with Iraq—which we did, six weeks after his UN speech.

The key reason why General Powell's legacy could have been tarnished—no one was ever able to find any WMD in Iraq.

How did General Powell respond? He easily could have blamed the CIA for inaccurate intelligence or others for pushing less than credible sources upon him, but he didn't. Instead, he took the blame himself, specifically stating within his 2012 published memoir: "I am mad mostly at myself for not having smelled the problem. My instincts failed me...It was by no means my first, but it was one of my most momentous failures, the one with the widest-ranging impact."[9]

I recall watching this unfold before the world and immediately saw him as a Level 5 public servant and leader. I often reflect on and admire how General Powell handled that situation, using a mirror versus a window to apportion responsibility for the war in Iraq. He owned it, exemplifying why he is considered one of the greatest leaders of our generation.

As a leader, you must sign a leadership declaration of interdependence with the teams you lead. You are only as good as those that support you, and any success you may achieve should be directly and immediately transferred to them. You and they are inextricably linked, and you should never lose sight of this. You cannot succeed without them, and you will most certainly fail without them. That same declaration also requires you as a leader to accept more of the blame when challenges arise. This, too, comes with leadership responsibility, and you must be willing and able to accept this, no matter the potential tarnish.

In my thirty-four-plus years of professional development, I have determined one of the quickest ways for a leader to lose the respect of those they lead is to accept more of the credit and less of the blame.

CHAPTER 29

Smell the Problem and Act

Whatever you do, you need courage. Whatever course you decide upon, there is always someone to tell you you are wrong. There are always difficulties arising which tempt you to believe that your critics are right. To map out a course of action and follow it to an end, requires some of the same courage which a soldier needs. Peace has its victories, but it takes brave men to win them.

—RALPH WALDO EMERSON

MANY HAVE SAID our greatest lessons learned come from our greatest failures. Assuming that to be true, I learned a lifetime of lessons in twelve of the most difficult months of my professional career in 2004. I experienced these hard lessons because of my own leadership failures that brought about an avalanche of challenges. This experience highlighted for me that courage is one of, if not the, most important leadership characteristics to own.

I was approached early in 2003 with an opportunity to develop a new business for Hewitt to be built around a team in Orlando. I was humbled and excited to begin building this business that would ultimately be called YSA, Hewitt's foray into the world of flexible-spending administration. Hewitt had been asked by clients for years to provide this service, and our business leadership finally felt the time was right to do so.

As with any new venture, there are an initial set of strategic decisions to be made that set the course for the business. These critical decisions have significant downstream implications on both successes and challenges. It is incumbent upon the leader to gather the necessary inputs from others to weigh those decisions, but it is ultimately the leader who must have the courage to make the right decisions—and often do so in the face of significant pressure. Unfortunately for YSA, our team members, and our clients, at each of those forks in the road, I chose the wrong direction even though I knew in my heart I should consider the alternative path.

I went 0-4 on these critical decisions, and our clients and team felt it.

I learned a great deal from these four failed decisions. While each decision was independent of the other, the common thread was my inability to have the courage to stand firm in the face of pressure and make the difficult decisions.

I have found it therapeutic to frequently reflect on these four errors and have shared them openly throughout my career. These failed decisions were as follows:

- **DECISION 1**: Initial claim processing in India. Hewitt had made a significant investment to open an office in India and was encouraging leaders across the organization to utilize this new, lower-cost alternative. As YSA was operating in a lower-margin industry and had no existing processes or teams to disrupt, it was strongly recommended we use the Hewitt India office to process our spending-account claims. The trouble with this design is we had not yet processed these claims in the United States, which meant we would be trying to perfect a process for the first time, from a distance of eight thousand miles. As you could imagine, this decision was ill-fated.
- **DECISION 2**: Initial call center in India. Similar to the above, when it was time to staff the YSA call center, it was strongly recommended we use the team in India. Hewitt leadership was

looking to direct call volume overseas, and we were encouraged to be among the first. If you're seeing a pattern here, you are not wrong. Mistake number two.

- DECISION 3: Debit card in v1 versus v2. Back in 2003, there was (at that time) cutting edge technology that would allow a customer to purchase healthcare items via an FSA debit card. Only a small number of competitors were offering this innovation and most all were offering it in a pilot fashion. Our original plan was to have this technology available in version 2 or 3 (mid-2004 or 2005) after we had perfected the foundational elements of YSA (claim admin, claim processing, website functionality). We were six months into our development schedule when the Hewitt client council strongly recommended we build this new functionality into our v1 software to increase the business opportunity. Yup, you guessed it, poor decision number three.

- DECISION 4: Limited beta test. As with any software development, you generally want to have a period of beta testing where you allow a smaller subset of customers to test out the platform, find the bugs, and enhance the product. You'll note that I used the term generally above—we ran short on time for several of the reasons noted above and launched the product without fully beta testing the software. We missed the opportunity to release our canary in a coal mine. Additionally, there was such a positive response to our proposed product and the inclusion of the FSA debit card out of the chute, that we had over twenty-five clients and 130,000 employee customers sign up to launch with us on January 1, 2004. Of course, included in that list of twenty-five clients were some of Hewitt's largest and most important outsourcing customers (including the firm's largest outsourcing client that shall remain nameless), which only intensified the situation. This final poor decision of mine was the nail in the coffin and set our launch toward a less-than-ideal outcome.

The good news is that time heals all wounds. The bad news is that it took us nearly twelve months to bandage up those wounds to the point they could effectively heal.

As I've now had time to reflect on these four poor decisions, I've come to appreciate the role of courage in leadership. With each of the above considerations, I knew the right answer was to push back on launching a new process in India, I knew we should stick to our original development plan and not significantly pivot on the fly, and I knew a smaller launch would set us up for better success. However, I felt this overwhelming and conflicting force to push forward, agree with firm leadership, agree with the client council, and launch the product so we could enjoy short-term success and capitalize on the market opportunity. Upon reflection, I now realize I lacked the courage to push against these market and internal forces, lacked the courage to prioritize the long term over the short-term, and lacked the courage to stand firm in my beliefs. It was a difficult lesson to learn, but I am better for having suffered through it and to have achieved clarity on the other side.

Reflective leadership requires us to learn from all of our experiences—both the good and the bad.

We have three potential outcomes when we are tested with adversity: we can become weakened, we can become hardened, or we can allow the adversity to transform us. I highly recommend a book by Jon Gordon and Damon West called *The Coffee Bean*, which is a fable about how we react to difficult situations and uses a carrot, egg, and a coffee bean to illustrate the stark differences. When faced with adversity, we can be like a carrot that weakens in a pot of boiling water, or we could be like an egg that hardens in the same environment. Alternatively, we can be like a coffee bean and positively transform the environment around us. Through the adversity our team faced in 2004, my choice was to learn from the situation and grow as a leader—to be a coffee bean.

Everyone on the YSA team worked harder than we had to, worked significantly more hours than we anticipated, took reputational hits, and lost a good bit of sleep. However, we also learned how to deal with challenging client situations and learned about adapting and overcoming obstacles. I, in particular, learned the invaluable lesson of the importance of courage in a leader and our need to transform our environment when faced with adversity.

It is these lessons learned, above all else, that I will remember from that first year of YSA.

Throughout my career, I have been on an aspirational journey to approach Level 5 Leadership, as highlighted in the book *Good to Great*. In this 2004 YSA situation, I needed to use a mirror and not a window to assign blame. To borrow the previous chapter's quote from General Powell, "I am mad mostly at myself for not having smelled the problem. My instincts failed me...It was by no means my first, but it was one of my most momentous failures."

My hope for you is that when you are faced with difficult decisions you recognize the need for courage and you call upon it. I can guarantee you it won't be easy to stand firm in your beliefs, but you and your team will be better for it.

CHAPTER 30

When the Storm Comes, Be a Buffalo

By three methods we may learn wisdom: First, by reflection, which is noblest; Second, by imitation, which is easiest; and third by experience, which is the bitterest.

—CONFUCIUS

THROUGHOUT MY CAREER and life, I have encountered more storms than I care to remember. Some of these storms have slowed me, most have battered me, yet all have shaped me. Just as in life, we can't control the weather or the storms that pass through our towns—they're omnipresent and driven by forces beyond our control. In a personal or professional setting, what can be controlled is how you respond to the storms as they approach or are upon you. You can either attempt to run away from the storm or you can charge headfirst into the brunt of the storm and aggressively take it on.

The conscious decisions we make when encountering a personal or professional storm are manifested daily on the high plains of Colorado by the cow and the buffalo. I first heard of the stark differences between these two animals during a church sermon, but it wasn't until I found myself in the midst of a professional storm that the metaphor truly resonated, and I was faced with a decision whether I was going to respond as a cow or a buffalo.

Upon relocating from New Jersey to Orlando with Hewitt in 1997, my family was confronted with the usual decisions tied to a move, including schooling, shopping, and places of worship. For the latter, we started attending a local Episcopal Church in Winter Park called All Saints, whose Rector at the time was a great man named Fr. David Wilson. Fr. Dave was a Naval Academy graduate and former helicopter pilot, so I had an immediate connection and respect for him. He hailed from the beautiful state of Colorado, and many of his sermons were based upon stories from growing up in a state with such varied topography.

One particular sermon has stayed with me over the years, and I frequently reflect upon its message in both personal and professional settings. The story revolves around people's reactions to challenging situations and employs an analogy that vividly contrasts the differences in how a cow and a buffalo respond to an approaching storm in Colorado. When cattle sense or see a storm coming over the Rockies from the west, the cows turn to the east and try to outrun the storm. Yet anyone who has ever witnessed a cow run knows this is a futile effort. Consequently, when the storm ultimately catches up to the cow, the poor bovine has simply elongated time in the tempest, unknowingly maximizing the amount of pain, time, and frustration they will experience within the storm. Buffalo, on the other hand, sense the same storm and charge west, propelling themselves forward at a thirty-five-mile-per-hour clip directly into the brunt of the approaching storm. By running headfirst into the storm, at a pace far quicker than the cow, the buffalo sprint straight through it, minimizing the amount of pain, time, and frustration they will experience from the same storm. Both animals have identical amounts of time to assess the situation, yet their responses to and experiences from the same storm are dramatically different.

In 2004, I found myself in the midst of one of the most severe storms of my professional career. As highlighted in the previous chapter, the ferocity of that storm was self-inflicted, and I found myself being battered like an untethered boat in a hurricane. To say that year was a struggle would be a gross understatement. It was both painful and frustrating, and there seemed to be no end to the storm. I couldn't outrun it, as hard as I tried. I found myself running east with the cows.

In that same year, I attended a Hewitt leadership event in Chicago. About midway through the leadership training, I sat up a little straighter, leaned into the lessons, and made a significant number of notes in the margin of our training materials. Toward the end of the session, I had an epiphany, and wrote three simple, yet powerful, words at the top of the page: "Be a Buffalo!"

Upon my return from Chicago, with a heavily annotated training binder, I shifted the weight from my heels to my toes. I met with members of our YSA leadership team, and we began aggressively attacking the issues we were facing, pushing the team to find solutions to our challenges, being more assertive with our partners, and owning the issues with our customers. It took some time to build momentum as our team began charging into the teeth of the YSA storm, but we began to see progress and daily wins were beginning to add up. The team could feel it, as could our customers.

The entire YSA team ultimately found our way through the storm by charging west, attacking challenges head-on with speed and precision. We knew our way out, and our collective energies buoyed us.

The shift in mindset that originated with a reflection on Fr. Dave's sermon was significant, both in helping our team get through the storm quicker and serving as a constant reminder of the right way to attack a professional storm—as a buffalo.

I have also found this metaphor to be helpful in personal storms. Whether it is a personal relationship that has hit hard times or a health challenge that initially seems insurmountable—these storms can batter and beat us down. These types of challenges can cause us to metaphorically attempt to outrun the storm in hopes we can outlast it, often to no avail. At the end of the day, there is one variable over which we have full control, and that is our mindset and how we choose to attack a storm.

In a professional setting, you must understand that leadership has no neutral action—you must take or push for action. Every action, no matter how small, contributes to either the success or detriment of the team or business you are leading. By running with the cows, you are not only prolonging the challenges you are facing within your storm, but you are also setting a poor example for your team in how they should conduct themselves and approach their work. Conversely, when you charge like a buffalo directly into the teeth of a storm, taking the challenge head-on, you not only help the team get through the situation sooner but also serve as an example for your team on how to manage their work and their lives.

Be a buffalo.

CHAPTER 31

Leadership Is a Muscle; It Requires Exercise

Good business leaders create a vision, articulate
the vision, passionately own the vision, and
relentlessly drive it to completion.
—JACK WELCH

C OUNTLESS STUDIES HAVE shown that exercise improves
nearly every aspect of our health: boosting sleep, strength,
and mental well-being while dramatically reducing the risk
of chronic conditions and premature death. Although the benefits
of exercise are well documented, the vast majority of Americans do
not engage in the recommended amount of daily physical activity.

Why is there such an incongruence of knowledge and action?
Because exercise is hard. If it was easy, everyone would do it.

If we're being honest, in today's instant gratification culture, if
the benefits of physical activity were made available in a pill, everyone would be clamoring to get the prescription filled at Walgreens.
Fortunately or unfortunately, no such pill exists, and so we're faced
with putting in the hard work to obtain the known benefits.

While it is difficult to build a level of fitness, it is even harder to
maintain it. There have been countless scientific studies that show
even the most elite athletes lose their level of fitness (e.g., decreased
glycogen storage) within a few weeks to a month of not exercising
their heart, lungs, or other muscles. Conversely, the weekend warrior

who opts to run, work out, or play pickleball once a month will have a hard time ever achieving or sustaining a level of fitness that generates the noted long-term health benefits. The body's muscles, especially the heart, require some degree of consistent exercise to reap the benefits. There are no shortcuts.

Leadership is no different. It is like a muscle that requires consistent exercise. If you wish to lead, you must be disciplined, and you must be consistent. Much like exercise, you simply cannot expect to experience gains by going to a leadership training event once a year or reading *Harvard Business Review* articles once a quarter. That would be akin to going to the YMCA for a singular weekend with a hope to become fit. It simply doesn't work.

Much like exercise, as a leader, you must consistently train, you must frequently apply leadership principles, and you must continually share your vision and hold people accountable. It is the little leadership acts that are performed every single day that build habit and muscle memory, not the once-a-year rah-rah speech or fancy vision statement. Creating and sharing the obligatory annual objectives without consistent application and management of them is like the fitness-oriented New Year's resolutions—proclamations without results. Much like fitness, there are no leadership shortcuts. There is no leadership pill.

Both exercise and leadership require significant discipline, consistency, and an "infinite mindset."

This infinite mindset was introduced to me by Simon Sinek, an outstanding author and speaker. Simon states that finite games, like football or chess, have known players, fixed rules, and a clear endpoint. The winners and losers are easily identifiable. In infinite games, like business, fitness, or life itself, the players come and go, the rules are changeable, and there is no defined endpoint. There are no winners or losers in an infinite game; there is only ahead and behind. If we try to lead people and businesses using a finite mindset within an infinite game, we will most certainly falter. Leading with an infinite mindset is crucial to an organization's long-term success.

For me, the best example of watching the leadership muscle consistently being exercised and leading with an infinite mindset was when I worked with Chris Gardner, CEO of HUB International Florida. Chris was charged with operating and leading within an acquisitive organization (fourteen acquisitions in nine years), with explosive growth (400 percent growth in those same nine years), and working to integrate disparate pieces (approximately twenty-five former business owners who were used to calling their own shots). Suffice to say, getting everyone to sing from the same hymnal was no small feat. It required discipline and consistency.

For Chris, it started with a vision. He set his vision for the organization back in 2015, and then he personally and consistently reinforced this vision in daily activities—via weekly, biweekly, or monthly integration/leadership calls, or some combination of these. Trust me: no one (especially Chris) woke up each Monday excited to attend a host of internal meetings aimed at ensuring the vision was clear and people were held accountable for their daily responsibilities. It was not easy and there were some days when it felt as though progress was not being made. However, just like exercise, not many people are excited to go to the gym Monday at 6:00 a.m., and not every workout feels like it makes a significant difference in your march toward fitness. It is about consistency and building muscle memory. Both leadership and maintaining fitness are hard. Both require discipline and consistency.

My encouragement for you is to exercise your leadership muscles today, tomorrow, next week, and beyond. Find a leadership blog you enjoy reading and read it daily. Subscribe to a leadership podcast and listen to it regularly. Be disciplined in hosting your leadership meetings—don't skip them or breeze through them. Consistently network with leaders outside of your organization. Continually share your vision and hold people accountable, especially yourself.

Leadership isn't easy, and it may not always be fun, but there are no shortcuts. Leadership requires significant discipline, consistency, and an infinite mindset, and I'm thankful I've been associated with leaders who have made this a priority and have successfully modeled this behavior for all.

Just like fitness, the long-term benefits are worth it.

CHAPTER 32

JGID

A shepherd should smell like his sheep.
—POPE FRANCIS

M Y ALMA MATER is known for having a very strong, and broadly successful, athletic program, with most every sport claiming a team or individual national championship at some point in the last twenty years—football, basketball, baseball, soccer, tennis, golf, softball, swimming, and gymnastics. However, within that time period, there is one sport that stands above the rest as having accumulated fourteen team national championships and ninety-five individual national champions—track and field.

The head coach of the Gators track and field program during this unprecedented run is a man by the name of Mike (Mouse) Holloway. Coach Holloway has mastered the art and science of being able to identify talent, assess cultural fit, motivate, train, and ensure his athletes are in peak condition at the right time—championship season. He is widely regarded as one of the greatest track and field coaches of his time—coaching not only NCAA champions, but also coaching professional athletes to Olympic medals, world championships, and world records. One of the greatest tips of the cap he's received is when he was asked to be the Head Coach for the 2020 US Olympic Track and Field team. I'm not one to assign the GOAT moniker too freely, but he's clearly in the conversation for track and field coaches.

I share all this with you, not because I am proud of my alma mater, but because one of my Reflection Collections comes from Coach Holloway, albeit from two different sources, with two related variations, and two decades apart.

The lesson I've borrowed from Coach Holloway is entitled JGID, and it stands for *just get it done.*

My second son, Jesse, was fortunate enough to run for Coach Holloway at UF from 2016 to 2021 and then joined his coaching staff upon graduation. As a result, I have had a front-row seat to witnessing Coach Holloway win many of those national titles and have had the unique opportunity to get to know him and hear many of his stories through Jesse. Each year, Coach Holloway creates a team mantra to motivate the team and galvanize them around a common goal. To that end, he annually creates a team T-shirt that everyone wears to serve as a constant reminder of that year's motto.

I believe the year was 2017, and Jesse came home wearing a T-shirt with the letters JGID across the back. Having no immediate recollection of the acronym, I had Jesse explain it to me. Jesse described it in very simple terms—no whining, no excuses, no BS—just get it done. Coach Holloway expects excellence in everything the team does, and he spurs the team on with the mentality of JGID.

Jesse's T-shirt ultimately broke free a memory that was deeply embedded within my brain and reminded me I had previously heard the JGID term before, and it was also related to UF Athletics. A good friend of mine, Rob Haddad, graduated a few years before me at UF and, upon graduation, went to work for the university in several capacities—working within the president's office and athletic association. During his time at UF, Rob became good friends with Jeremy Foley, UF's athletic director. Jesse's shirt reminded me of a story Rob shared regarding Jeremy and a unique leadership philosophy he held—JGID.

As Rob tells the story, he and Jeremy attended a UF tennis match in the early 1990s and were casually sitting in the stands, enjoying the match. At some point, as is often the case on a Florida summer day, it started to rain, and they suspended the match to allow the rain to pass. Once the rain subsided, the tennis crew began working to get the courts ready to restart the matches, but they clearly needed help as they appeared to be short-handed that day. Without saying a word, Jeremy grabbed Rob, and the two of them leaped from the stands to help the crew squeegee the courts to remove any standing water. Once the task was successfully completed and as they returned to their seats, Rob asked why, as athletic director, he would leave the stands to perform a task someone else was surely able to do. Jeremy's response was rather simple—JGID. Jeremy held firm to a belief that no one is above anyone else, and there is never a situation where the words "that's not my job" should be uttered.

Jeremy used the JGID mentality throughout his twenty-four-year tenure as athletic director for the University as he built a strong culture of teamwork, accountability, and humility. For Jeremy, the JGID mentality served as a constant reminder that no one was above what he called "the Place." In his case, the Place was the University of Florida Athletics and he considered himself but a momentary steward. It is this type of humility that allowed him to move toward Level 5 Leadership. When Jeremy retired in 2016, he was widely regarded as one of, if not the, greatest athletic directors in the country.

I loved working with leaders who had no qualms with leaping from their proverbial stands to squeegee the courts, and I worked diligently to do the same for the teams I led. I appreciated leaders who led by example and dirtied their hands along the way, willing to work side by side with any member of their team, regardless of rank.

Pope Francis once said, "A shepherd should smell like his sheep," and I strived to live and lead by that concept most of my career. In leading this way, it demonstrates a leader does not view themselves as being above any activity, and if someone on their team is counted on to perform a task, the leader should be willing to do the same. For the teams I led, I worked tirelessly to eradicate the phrase "it's not my job" from their vocabularies, and I tried to lead by example in this regard.

JGID was on constant display throughout my time at Hewitt Associates. Every leader was willing, able, and eager to leap from the stands to squeegee a court. This was never more evident than during employee benefits open enrollment season—when Hewitt would establish call centers to help our clients enroll employees in their benefit programs. Now, keep in mind the majority of Hewitt's clients were among the Fortune 500, which meant staffing a call center for millions of customers was no small feat. We employed several industrial engineers to perfect the staffing models and ensure we had sufficient people available to answer the phones during peak volumes.

At the end of the day, Hewitt employed their own version of JGID called "all hands on deck" (AHOD). For select windows of time, Hewitt would reach deep into their bench and ask non-call-center employees (technology, administrative, and leadership types) to jump on the phones for a day or two to help mitigate the volume pressures on days with the highest call-volume forecast. This AHOD/JGID mentality underscored and amplified the focus on teamwork, humility, and shared accountabilities that was prevalent throughout the Hewitt organization.

Now, that said, defined roles and responsibilities are clearly necessary within any team. There should be a squeegee crew ready to clear the courts when the time comes. However, when the team needs help, every person on that team, particularly the leaders, should be willing and able to jump in to enthusiastically lend a hand to just get it done.

When you have the opportunity to lead, I strongly suggest you adopt the JGID mentality, not just for yourself, but for all members of your team. You must lead from the front on this and be an example to others. I also urge you to be alert and consistently tune your frequency as opportunities for growth can be found in the simplest places, such as your child's T-shirt.

Whichever moniker you place on this mentality (JGID or AHOD), the end result is the same—a team that encourages humility, teamwork, and shared accountabilities (and no whining/BS) will outperform those that do not.

This team-oriented philosophy was clearly on display throughout Jeremy Foley's time at the helm of UF Athletics. There, he smelled like his sheep, won twenty-seven national titles, and hired some of the greatest coaches in UF's history: Billy Donnovan, Urban Myer, and, you guessed it, Mike Holloway.

JGID.

CHAPTER 33

Force Multipliers Are a Double-Edged Sword—Choose Wisely

Keep your face always toward the sunshine—
and shadows will fall behind you.
—WALT WHITMAN

I HAVE NEVER BEEN someone who posts a lot on social media, and so I am intentional about what I post and about whom I post. As a case in point, I have only twice posted about a nonrelative's death. In those instances, their passing has shaken me to my core, as if losing them felt as though I was losing a family member. Those two individuals are, Stuart Scott (ESPN personality) and General Colin Powell (four-star general, national security adviser, chairman of the Joint Chiefs of Staff, and secretary of state). I always loved Stuart Scott's voice, his humor, his wit, and his spirit. I could rewatch any SportsCenter segment or speech he gave and be glued to the screen, entranced by his words, and uplifted by his energy. As it relates to General Powell, I consider him one of the greatest leaders of my lifetime and someone I held in the highest regard.

Being someone with an affinity for the military, I had always been aware of General Powell and the role he was playing within our armed forces. However, he became more than just a military hero for me when I was introduced to Dr. Oren Harari's book *The Leadership Secrets of Colin Powell*, easily one of the most influential leadership books of our generation. If you've not yet had the opportunity to read it, I highly recommend you do. The book is strikingly practical and refreshingly honest.

In the introduction of this book, I highlighted how I identified with Lou Gehrig due to our shared humble beginnings and commitment to hard work, which served as an early inspiration for me. Similarly, General Powell's humble origins and strong work ethic resonated with me as an adult, becoming a source of further inspiration. As a result, I avidly tracked his career and absorbed any material related to his life. The impact *The Pride of the Yankees* had on my formative years was complemented by *The Leadership Secrets of Colin Powell* in my professional years. It was in Dr. Harari's book that I first heard of force multipliers being used within a professional context.

The term *force multiplier* is a military term that refers to any factor that enhances the effectiveness and capabilities of something beyond its inherent capabilities. It allows a smaller force to have a disproportionately larger impact. In a professional world, a force multiplier has a similar effect—it constructively enhances the effectiveness and capabilities of a team or organization. However, it is important to acknowledge that destructive force multipliers such as toxicity and negativity can be equally as powerful and uniquely harmful to an organization.

One of the chapters in Dr. Harari's book talks about the impact optimism played in General Powell's leadership. His quote was actually, "Perpetual Optimism is a Force Multiplier."[10] What General Powell meant is that a leader's positive and optimistic outlook can have a significant and amplifying effect on an individual's or a team's effectiveness and accomplishments. I watched a video of General Powell dissecting the details of this quote. He shared that while in infantry school, he was instructed, "No matter how cold it is, [Lieutenant], you must never look cold. No matter how hungry you are, you must never appear hungry. No matter how terrified you are, you must never look terrified." As a leader, he understood that a motivated team is more likely to overcome a challenge, and so he knew he would have to maintain an optimistic outlook to motivate his troops. Finally, he knew that optimism is contagious, and an optimistic leader can influence and uplift those around him or her, creating a ripple effect throughout a team and organization.

When I first launched MillsonJames, I was in a men's group with my friend, colleague, and mentor, John Rivers. As noted previously, John had just the year prior opened 4 Rivers Smokehouse, a wildly successful and rapidly growing BBQ business throughout Florida, and I had come alongside him to offer help on the people side of his business.

One day when John and I were visiting one of the Smokehouses, he shared with me that any time he arrived at a store and began interacting with the staff, he could predict the mood of the store's GM. If the staff was mulling about, just getting work done, and displaying low energy, he could guess the GM wasn't having a great day and may be in a foul mood. Conversely, if the staff was bouncing about with high energy and excited to start the day, he would predict the GM was in a good mood and was setting the right tone. This predictive model proved to be true most every time, and it served as a great lesson and reminder for me that leadership is a force multiplier. The leader sets the tone for everyone else, and they control how that power is used. John and I shared this axiom at most every GM meeting—be positive, have high energy, be optimistic—because the team was watching and following their lead.

As a leader, you must understand that you are a force multiplier, and you need to be mindful of how you're reacting to situations, responding to various stimuli, and projecting emotions. If you are calm, your team will be calm. If you project chaos, your team will be chaotic. If you are openly frustrated by a situation, your team will become frustrated. You must be like a duck swimming in a pond. The duck appears to be gliding on the surface of the water even though they are paddling like mad beneath the surface. Don't let your team see you sweat or how madly you're paddling.

The US Navy SEALs refer to this very concept as "calm is contagious." Given the daily chaos they often encounter and the success they frequently achieve, we would do well to follow this mantra.

I have experienced leaders who were exceptional at both ends of the peace/chaos spectrum, positively and negatively. I've seen leaders who were in the midst of a professional hurricane, and you'd think they were sitting in a church service. Conversely, I've seen leaders who were visibly angry and openly frustrated when faced with a springtime rain shower. When you're leading a team, I encourage you to emulate the former and not the latter.

It should be noted I'm not suggesting a leader should be a Pollyanna, ignoring obvious perils that may exist. An optimist is someone who expects positive outcomes, yet that optimism is grounded in a realistic assessment of the situation. Being a perpetual optimist isn't about being naive to potential problems. It is about a choice to inject positivity into the situation and team, for the good of the team. Conversely, pessimists have no hope for a positive outcome and will unfortunately succumb to the weight of that chosen negativity.

Always keep in mind that "no matter how cold it is, [Lieutenant], you must never look cold."

The teams you lead will appreciate your calming influence and leveraging your force multiplier to be constructive as opposed to destructive.

In the words of Stuart Scott, "Booyah!"

CHAPTER 34

Empower the Front Line

The greatest enemy of knowledge is not
ignorance, it is the illusion of knowledge.
—STEPHEN HAWKING

I HAVE A GREAT deal of respect for heights. Some might call it an unhealthy respect. Heck, some might label it as an outright fear—and they wouldn't be wrong. I'm not entirely sure from where my acrophobia emanates, but it is unfortunately lurking beneath the surface anytime I am exposed to the elements and at a height above fifty feet. I'm quite comfortable on an airplane but put me on the Eiffel Tower's outdoor observation deck, and I'm a wreck. I wish it weren't the case, but it is a reality.

This healthy dose of acrophobia most certainly means I won't be climbing any mountains or hiking high-altitude trails anytime soon. Although I would absolutely love the scenic outlooks or the exhilaration of reaching a summit, I'm a realist and know that my fears would win out and I'd be returning to basecamp much sooner than I'd like. This also means I will never formally use the skills of a sherpa, a mountain guide that helps climbers safely ascend a mountain. Sherpas are renowned in the international climbing and mountaineering community for their knowledge and experience at very high altitudes. They have developed an unparalleled level of expertise about their region, and any climber with an ounce of intelligence and perspective would gladly use them to help summit their chosen mountain.

Although I have never formally met a sherpa, I have met thousands of them along my professional journey, and you have or will too. In a professional setting, I define sherpa as anyone who has developed a level of expertise with a task by living and grinding it daily. They are on the front lines and know their job inside and out. They are also subject-matter experts and should be looked upon to influence change or make decisions, but too often, they aren't utilized by the very leaders who are charged with guiding them.

Unfortunately, within most every organization throughout the United States, there is an inverse and unhealthy relationship between power and information. The leaders at the top of an organizational chart have all the power and limited information, and the employees at the bottom of the organizational chart have all the information and no power to effect or implement change. Successful leaders must find a way to ensure information flows freely from the front lines to produce the desired balance of power and information.

This is not unlike the experience of a mountain climber.

As a mountain climber ascends toward their summit, the air becomes thinner, the trails become more treacherous, and the difference between success and failure is razor thin. Clearly, the climber needs information and guidance to achieve their objective. However, there will be climbers who allow their ego to get in the way and press onward, trying to reach the summit by themselves and without critical information. On the other hand, successful climbers recognize and appreciate their climb can only be successful if they tap into the information and experience of those living in the area and who have deep appreciation for the region—a sherpa. When a climber calls upon their sherpas, their likelihood of success increases exponentially. The same holds true in a professional setting for when a leader successfully leverages their version of sherpas—their team on the front lines—success is right around the corner.

I have fortunately been around leaders who understood their success was inextricably linked to their teams and were exceptional at gathering information from the experts—those living and grinding in the daily details. These leaders have worked hard to level out the aforementioned power/information imbalance as they have granted authority down the organizational chart and encouraged information to float up.

There are two extraordinary examples of this that I encountered fairly early in my career, and I have utilized both multiple times with the teams I've led.

The first came from Delta Airlines and how they encouraged information to float upward in the early 1990s. As a recession began to blanket the United States, employers were actively looking to reduce waste and find efficiencies. Many employers hired expensive consultants to identify elaborate ways to improve margins. Delta took a different approach. They understood the people best suited to provide the executive team with cost-cutting suggestions were not a bunch of high-priced external consultants but rather the employees on the front lines of their business, those living in the trenches and interacting daily with their customers. Their sherpas.

They launched an internal campaign encouraging cost-cutting suggestions to float up from the front lines. The suggestions they received from their team were insightful and impactful. The most noteworthy suggestion came from a flight attendant—and it saved Delta $1.8 million per year!

Some of you may recall the highly average airline meals that were an industry staple prior to 2001. In that time period, Delta had this custom of serving their side dishes of coleslaw, cottage cheese, or fruit salad ensconced within a large, single leaf of lettuce. The leaf of lettuce served no real purpose other than presentation.

This particular flight attendant noted that 95 percent of travelers on her flights discarded this leaf of lettuce without giving any thought to eating it. Her suggestion from the front line was to eliminate this leaf of lettuce from the meal, knowing it wouldn't be missed by the vast majority of Delta's passengers. Once tallied, this suggestion saved Delta Airlines tens of millions of dollars over the ensuing years. More importantly, it demonstrated to the Delta employees that leadership valued their input and wanted to find the balance of power and information.

I have leveraged this story and attempted to replicate its action several times over the last thirty-plus years. Although the organizations for whom I worked never identified a million-dollar leaf of lettuce suggestion, we were successful in encouraging ideas to be floated northward and helping employees recognize that leadership appreciated and respected their knowledge and experience.

When we first opened the Hewitt Orlando office in 1997, we launched a campaign to encourage a free flow of information throughout the office, which we not surprisingly named "Leaf of Lettuce." We wanted to set a tone for that office and let our employees know how much we valued their knowledge, expertise, and innovation. The cost-cutting suggestions we received were secondary to the culture we established.

The second example came about from a keynote speaker who closed the 2002 Hewitt Associates Client Conference in Phoenix, Arizona. Hewitt asked retired US Navy captain Michael Abrashoff to speak at our conference and share details of his recently launched book, *It's Your Ship*. Captain Abrashoff shared several stories at the conference, but there was one story that came across loud and clear on his frequency of excellence, and I was fortunate to hear it. The story exemplified the importance of a leader to engage their front lines, and I have retold the story countless times.

Captain Abrashoff took command of the USS *Benfold*, a guided-missile destroyer, in the summer of 1997. Upon his arrival, the USS *Benfold* was among the lowest-performing ships in the Pacific Fleet. The challenges of this underachieving destroyer were staggering, with low morale and the highest turnover rate in the Navy. Few thought the ship could improve. Yet twelve months following Captain Abrashoff's arrival, it was ranked number one in performance—using the same crew.

How did he achieve such amazing and profound success in such a short period? You'll have to read his book to get the full story, but part of his approach was to open the communication doors and encourage information to float upward. As the new skipper, he recognized he was in unfamiliar territory, and while he had the power to effect change, he didn't have the necessary information from the people who were living and breathing the daily operations of the *Benfold*. He needed to call upon his team. His sherpas.

As he took command of the *Benfold*, he immediately began interviewing all 310 sailors aboard the *Benfold*. Five sailors a day, one at a time, seven days a week. He wanted to get to know them, and, more importantly, he wanted to open the lines of communication. During one of the interviews, a sailor highlighted his least favorite task as a crewmember—sanding and painting the ship, every other month, six times a year. As a lower-ranking sailor, this mundane responsibility fell to him and others like him, the lowest in the ship's chain of command. The sailor appreciated that while it was important to keep the *Benfold* looking shipshape, the hit to morale was significant and, in his eyes, unnecessary.

The fresh coat of paint was required bimonthly to cover the rust stains that came from the ferrous metals used by the Navy when constructing the ship. The sailor suggested that if they had used stainless steel bolts, there would be no rust and, hence, no need to sand and repaint every other month.[11]

Captain Abrashoff alone had the power to order replacement stainless steel nuts and bolts but lacked the information that would prompt him to do so. When this information was floated to him, he quickly acted and placed the order for thousands of dollars of stainless steel fasteners. Once the new fasteners were installed, the crew didn't have to repaint the *Benfold* for nearly a year! The morale of the sailors dramatically improved—not just because they could leave the paint brushes stowed in their lockers but also because Captain Abrashoff was actively listening to them. By opening the lines of communication and encouraging upward communication, he leveled out the balance of power and information.

It was simple actions like this that allowed the USS *Benfold* to become the number one ship in the Pacific Fleet.

This story has stuck with me for over twenty years and has served as a perfect example of how to utilize your team to bring ideas from the front line.

Captain Abrashoff's success with the USS *Benfold* is replicable. All you need is a leader who is willing to level out the balance of power and information—someone who is willing to open the line of communications and someone who encourages and celebrates this behavior. That someone can be you if you simply never lose sight of the fact that the air becomes thinner as you ascend the corporate ladder. You must always leverage the people who have firsthand experience in working with your customers or your operations. They have the knowledge, experience, and expertise.

They are your sherpas and they can help you summit your chosen mountain.

Entrepreneurship

CHAPTER 35

Lock Down All Escape Hatches

The difference between involvement and commitment is like
ham and eggs. The chicken is involved; the pig is committed.
—MARTINA NAVRATILOVA

A S I SET out to launch MillsonJames in 2010, I actively
reached out to friends, colleagues, and mentors who were
business owners. My goal was to learn from their experiences,
test my ideas, and invite them to challenge my perspectives. These
outreaches were inspired by my father-in-law's advice to seek knowledge from individuals and authors who had encountered different
experiences than my own—a Wisdom Quest. I had a long list of
people with whom I wanted to meet, and I was never disappointed.
Whether knowingly or not, each person shared one or two pearls of
wisdom that served as a foundation for MillsonJames. One of these
outreaches was to a friend named Charles Tews, and our 2010 lunch
stands as one of the greatest thirty-dollar investments I've ever made.

A bit of backstory might be helpful to understand the impact of
Charles's pearl. Charles is the founder and CEO of Tews Company, an
Orlando-based recruiting and staffing firm. I reached out to Charles
to learn more about how he launched Tews, the successes he'd had,
and the challenges he'd overcome. However, if I'm being totally honest, I had a bit of a hidden agenda in meeting with Charles. Although
I was certain I was ready to leave my current employment situation
and launch MillsonJames, the little voice in the back of my head was

telling me to have a contingency plan just in case the business launch didn't go as I'd planned. During our lunch, I brought up to Charles that since his firm handled executive recruiting, I'd be grateful if he could keep me in mind for any high-level positions in the Orlando area, just in case. Charles's response was something I was not expecting yet became one of the best pieces of advice I've ever received.

"No. I will not do that."

After I picked myself off the floor and tried to conceal my bewilderment, he shared why he would not be sharing my resume with potential employers. He explained that as an entrepreneur, you must be all in, and you must lock down all escape hatches. He further illustrated that if you operate your new business knowing there is a possible out or an alternative path to take, then you will be diluting your focus and, ultimately, submarining your business.

Although it was not an answer I was expecting, he was spot on with that sage advice and his perspective fueled me and provided me with laser-like focus on the task at hand—building a successful business. Following that lunch, I was all in with MillsonJames, and I worked diligently to ensure all escape hatches were bolted and welded shut.

That encounter reminded me of a similar piece of advice provided by another friend, Kim Cullen, several years prior. Kim is an attorney who had left a larger firm in 2002 to launch his own practice. Around that time, Kim and I were training for a marathon, which meant we had hours upon hours to do nothing but stare at the pavement, sweat, and talk. On one of our longer training runs, I began picking his brain to understand his experiences in launching his business. His response was similar to what I learned from Charles a few years later. He shared that the level of commitment and love he had for his business was second only to the love he had for his family. That felt a little extreme at the time, but once I launched MillsonJames, I understood exactly what he was conveying on that run.

These two experiences served as a driving force for me when launching MillsonJames and I was appreciative of being tuned in at lunch with Charles and while running with Kim. I was all in on ensuring my business would be a successful venture. It also served as a reminder for me in life—that your actions will follow your beliefs, and if you have doubts about what you're doing or are constantly looking for an escape hatch, you are limiting the potential success of whatever it is you're doing.

Although I didn't initially tag it as such, I'm also grateful that Charles helped execute a Ulysses contract with respect to MillsonJames. With his sage advice and denial of my resume request, he was holding me accountable and was significantly increasing the likelihood of my firm's success. As referenced in an earlier chapter and rooted in Greek mythology, the war hero Ulysses knew he would be drawn to the beautiful Sirens living on an enchanted yet treacherous island and gave strict instructions to his ship's crew that they were to ignore any pleas he made to divert their ship toward the perilous shore. Charles essentially helped me execute a contract similar to the one between Ulysses and his crew by ignoring my request to keep an eye out for any new job openings.

I am eternally grateful not only for Charles and Kim's advice, but for them holding me accountable and setting MillsonJames up for success.

My encouragement for you is that if you are considering launching your own business, you are fully committed and in love. Infatuated, actually. Entrepreneurship is akin to a deep relationship as you will be pouring your heart and soul into it, and you must be willing to do whatever it takes to ensure the relationship (a.k.a. business) thrives.

The Spanish conquistador Hernán Cortés arrived in the New World in 1519 with a plan to conquer the Aztec Empire. His men were tired, weary from the travel, and not ready or willing to fight. Cortés recognized this and requested that the crew burn the boats they had just used to complete their voyage. This sent a clear message to his men—there was no turning back, and the only way forward was to succeed in their conquest or face defeat. In business terms, they needed to be all in and 100 percent committed. Two years later, he succeeded in his conquest of the Aztec Empire because of their determined resolve.

My hope is that when you launch your own business, you will be as committed as Hernán Cortés. I also hope you have good friends and family to remind you of the commitment required to be successful and hold you accountable.

Entrepreneurship takes a village—one with burned boats at the shore.

CHAPTER 36

Spousal/Partner Support Is Critical

Alone we can do so little; together we can do so much.
—HELEN KELLER

E LEANOR ROOSEVELT FAMOUSLY once said, "Behind every successful man, there is a strong woman," and she embodied that quote in her role as first lady. The partnership between a president and first lady and, recently, between a vice president and second gentleman, is absolutely critical in the leadership of our country. A great leader cannot exist without the unwavering support of others—whether it is the support of a wife to a husband, a husband to a wife, or a significant other to another, having that level of support is critical when tackling a challenging task. This is particularly true with an entrepreneurial endeavor when the starting point is zero—as in zero sales, zero revenue, zero salary.

While this may fall under the category of common sense for some, it was initially and, through reflection, repeatedly driven home for me with a simple three-word question asked of me by one of my mentors. In the mid-to-late 2000s, whenever I would come up with some new business idea or would desire a professional opinion, I would call John Bausch, a great friend and mentor from Hewitt/ Sageo. John was an exceptional listener and a brilliant mind, and I truly valued his opinion.

When I called to get his input on this MillsonJames business idea I had, he allowed me to run through my business plan and listened to my (long) list of desired outcomes and concerns. After I had finished my soliloquy, he paused and asked me one simple question, "Is Kristin aboard?"

I thought, *Did you not hear my great business idea? Surely, you can poke holes in it. Do you have any counterpoints to my points?* I even jokingly thought, *I called seeking your professional/career input, not marital advice.*

The genius in John's simple question wasn't soaked in business design, organizational development, or financial strategy, but it was heartfelt, and it was precisely on point. It took several repetitions of me calling John, John allowing me to brain dump, and John repeatedly asking me that simple question before it finally took root.

This question would soon become the first consideration of any future business idea I would dream up—Is Kristin aboard?

Mentally, I knew launching a new business or pivoting an existing business strategy would require me to be all in, locking down any escape hatches. However, it took a mentor to clearly remind me that I would not be in this start-up boat alone—that my beautiful and loving wife would be taking this leap of faith with me, and she would need to be all in as well.

The good news for me is that Kristin was already engaged and supportive of my professional goals and dreams. She was ready, willing, and excited to jump out of the airplane without a (then) functioning parachute. I'm not sure either of us knew exactly what "for better or for worse" meant when we exchanged vows in 1991, but we were ready to tackle the MillsonJames challenges—together.

Launching a business can be extraordinarily stressful as it places excessive financial, time, and energy demands on business owners and their spouses. In reality, the role of a "start-up spouse" can be even more daunting because the spouse is not in control of the day-to-day activities and may feel helpless in certain situations. To help ease this concern, I made it a point to involve her in every major decision of MillsonJames—whether to launch a new product, whether to take on a new client, or whether to reinvest back into the business—and she appreciated it. Certainly, having a spouse or significant other's support and guidance is critical to any career and at all levels, but I have found it is an imperative when working through the launch and growth of a start-up organization.

So the answer to John's important question of whether Kristin was aboard was and is an emphatic yes, and I would encourage any entrepreneur to ask themselves the same question before entering the launch codes. You will be setting yourself up for success, not only at your office, but also at home.

Any success I have been able to achieve as a professional, whether entrepreneurial or not, has come because of the strength of my most important partner.

I'm appreciative of my mentor for holding me accountable and to the former first lady for summing up my career so perfectly.

"Behind every successful man, there is a strong woman."

CHAPTER 37

Write Your Business Plan in Pencil

Everyone has a plan until they get punched in the mouth.
—MIKE TYSON

I F YOU SURVEYED one hundred entrepreneurs and asked them whether their initial business plan (if they even wrote one) played out as they originally envisioned, I'd venture a guess that darn near all hundred would respond to the negative. It is nearly impossible for an initial business plan to go according to plan because the only way to truly understand and experience the market challenges and successes you will face is to launch—and then get ready to be punched in the mouth, even if it is just a glancing blow.

It is the nature of the start-up beast.

When you're envisioning a business, you assume what the market will want, why they will want it, the value they will place on it, and how they will want it delivered. The operative word in the preceding sentence is *assume*. You may try to validate your initial assumptions via focus groups, market testing, and other various methods, but the only real way to test your hypotheses is to launch.

I have several firsthand experiences in learning this lesson as I've been fortunate to participate in several start-ups and business launches throughout my career. That said, this lesson was most effectively driven home for me during my time with Sageo, the Hewitt Associates spinoff I was lucky enough to be a part of back in 1999. With apologies to my former Hewitt partners, but in recognition and appreciation for the peaks and valleys that exist with any start-up, there were more twists and turns along the Sageo journey than the winding Hana Highway in Maui.

The Sageo business plan, as originally written during the ill-fated dot-com boom era, was for Hewitt to launch an e-business to create an online health exchange for retirees. We had market tested the business, built hundreds of pro formas, and had several start-up consultants guiding us along the way. We thought we knew what the market wanted and had a plan to get there—it was all about first-mover advantage, eyeballs on a website (foolishly dot-com driven), and serving an underserved market.

Then we launched—and the market informed us what they really wanted, and it was different than what we had originally planned. Throughout the year following our launch, I recall most every Sageo leadership team call was lively, full of debate, and oriented around change. It was maddening but necessary. There was no way to anticipate the punches that were coming our way—until we were standing in the ring waiting to get hit.

Whether you are launching a large-scale business or hanging out your own shingle, one of the most accurate predictors of success for an entrepreneur is adaptability/flexibility. Writing your business plan in pencil forces you to look at change as the only constant—make change your friend, embrace it, and work it to your benefit. Too often, an entrepreneur will hog-tie themselves to their original business plan, do everything possible to stay the initial course, and have a firm, yet unhealthy, belief in their initial assumptions.

This unfortunate form of "business plan worship" is one of the most accurate predictors of failure for an entrepreneur.

Ego serves as a double-edged sword in entrepreneurship. On one hand, a healthy ego can contribute to confidence and ambition, driving entrepreneurs to set high goals, take risks, and pursue aggressive visions for their businesses. Additionally, when times get tough (and they will), a certain level of ego can provide the necessary resilience to persist in the face of setbacks and criticism.

On the other hand, an unchecked ego can lead to stubbornness and resistance to changing strategies or adapting to new information. Entrepreneurs who are overly attached to their ideas may fail to see alternative, potentially more effective approaches. Ignoring feedback from partners, employees, customers, investors, or advisers may result in missed opportunities for improvement and innovation. Don't ever forget about your sherpas and be sure to use them to maintain the balance of power and information.

As it relates to writing a business plan, please don't misunderstand my message or my reflections of previous start-ups. I believe firmly in planning versus haphazardly winging it. Dwight D. Eisenhower famously once said, "In preparing for battle, I have always found that plans are useless, but planning is indispensable."

I highly encourage you to develop a plan to ensure you know where you are aiming. However, in your planning, do yourself a favor and be flexible with your plan and be ready to adapt to the unforeseen challenges. As time passes and initial assumptions are validated or invalidated, you will have a better sense for what the market wants and what they are willing to pay, how they want it delivered, and to whom they want it delivered. At that point, it is more than appropriate to begin narrowing the field of assumptions and consider writing your annual goals and objectives with more indelible ink.

Just be sure to start with a pencil.

CHAPTER 38

Trust the Process

Patience and perseverance have a magical effect before
which difficulties disappear and obstacles vanish.
—JOHN QUINCY ADAMS

BEING BORN AND originally raised in Chicago, I am a die-hard Chicago Cubs, Bears, Bulls, and Blackhawks fan. I have also successfully brainwashed my children into understanding the aforementioned teams are, hands down, the greatest franchises in all of sports. Because of this, I have no affinity for any teams residing outside the 312 area code, including the Philadelphia 76ers or any Philadelphia sports teams for that matter. However, I have come to appreciate, respect, and have successfully utilized the mantra of the 76ers General Manager Stan Hinkie—trust the process.

Stan Hinkie was hired by the Sixers in the spring of 2013 to less-than-favorable applause from Philadelphia fans. He was brought aboard to turn things around with the then-ailing franchise. When he was first introduced to the media, he made it abundantly clear he was going to do things differently and he would be making some bold moves, but there was a method to his madness. Essentially, he was asking, maybe proactively pleading, with the citizens of Philadelphia and their rabid fanbase to be patient and trust the process.

He was a man of his word, and he immediately began implementing his plan. He traded away star players for future draft picks, and the team began their anticipated free fall. He further irritated fans when he used a high draft pick to select an injured player named Joel Embiid. Hinkie knew Embiid would have to sit out a number of games in his first two seasons because of his injuries, but he remained resolute with the pick and encouraged everyone to trust the process.

Since Hinkie first attached that phrase to the 76ers' rebuilding process, it has also become a familiar rallying cry for any individual or organization hoping to encourage themselves, their employees, or their fan bases to be patient and to not lose their marbles if overnight success isn't attained. In a world characterized by instant gratification, social media, and information overload, leaders often find themselves overwhelmed by the pressure to produce immediate results. This is particularly true in the corporate arena, where quarterly results are king and private equity groups are eager for scheduled returns. The trust-the-process philosophy encourages a deliberate focus on the present, fostering a sense of purpose and intentionality in every action taken. By trusting the process, individuals can navigate future challenges with a calm-and-collected mindset.

I have leaned into this philosophy several times throughout my career, but it was on full display during the launch of MillsonJames. As an entrepreneur, you must be patient. The first few years of a launch are certain to be filled with more downs than ups, and you must recognize that your results may not immediately line up with your activities.

I have often reflected on one specific comment made to me by one of my mentors as I was considering the MillsonJames launch that not only underscored this philosophy, but also helped me maintain perspective. This comment served as my North Star throughout the trials of the first few years and was exceptionally accurate with its prediction.

The mentor's advice was to enter MillsonJames with a clear understanding that it would take two years to replace my previous executive salary.

Wait, what? Two full years?

That comment hit me hard and knocked me back a good bit. My left brain took over, and I quickly began doing the math, working to create a Millson family 2010–2011 pro forma in my head. As I began seeing a good bit of red ink in my mind, fear crept into the room, and I began to sweat. How would I pay for my children's education? Can we afford our current home? How can I even afford today's lunch? I left the discussion with my mentor a bit disheartened, but appreciative of the advice.

With this newfound perspective, I returned to my office and began crunching numbers, trying to find ways within Excel to expedite revenue and diminish costs. After a few hours of this frantic exercise, I took a deep breath and walked away, recognizing that Excel can often produce fool's gold for an entrepreneur—you can make any situation seem rosier by simply adjusting numbers within a cell. What I realized during my time away from the computer is that I needed to trust the process. Even more so, my mentor's advice gave me an awareness and a confidence I could weather the financial storms of MillsonJames if I just stuck with the process, believed in what I was doing, and didn't get caught up in the red ink of any given month. Trust me: there were many months when our family struggled, but Kristin and I believed in MillsonJames and trusted in our process to make it a resounding success.

Beyond the numbers, trust the process also helped me appreciate that success would not happen overnight. Success, however you'd like to define it, was going to take time and would require a good bit of resilience and adaptability. This mentality helped me understand and appreciate that entrepreneurship is inherently unpredictable—setbacks would be inevitable. By trusting the MillsonJames process, I was able to view challenges as opportunities for growth and didn't become discouraged by any obstacles that fell before me. Taking things one day at a time, one week at a time, and one month at a time afforded me the ability to be patient and find opportunities in challenges, ultimately understanding that any short-term setback was just that—a short-term setback.

Although MillsonJames launched three years before Stan Hinkie uttered the phrase *trust the process*, I embraced the mentality and have called upon this reflection often. I vowed to learn from the challenges and embrace a growth mindset, viewing setbacks as stepping stones toward success. This steadfast trust in my process helped position myself and the organization for continuous improvement and sustainable, long-term achievement. There were no quarterly earnings targets for me to hit and no private equity partners to satisfy with a quick return. I lived in the present and happily took a step forward each and every day, trusting in our process, much like Stan Hinkie.

Alas, the Philadelphia 76ers have not yet won their championship, but a great foundation has been laid, including an MVP award for Joel Embiid.

Both of those recent results are unfortunately more than I can say for my beloved Chicago Bulls.

(I can only hope that they have a process in which I can trust.)

SECTION 7

Career Advice

CHAPTER 39

The Name on the Front of Your Jersey Is as Important as the Back

If people like you, they will listen to you; but if they trust you, they'll do business with you.

—ZIG ZIGLAR

ONE OF MY all-time favorite sports movies is *Miracle*, the story of the US Men's Winter Olympic Hockey Team that shocked the world and won the gold medal in 1980. The movie is full of great characters, the storyline is inspiring, and it stirs within me a patriotic nostalgia I recall feeling as a thirteen-year-old boy.

The Olympic matchup between the United States and the Soviet Union was particularly significant against the backdrop of the Cold War, as the two nations were not only political but also economic, social, and athletic rivals. Suffice to say, there was not a lot of love between the two countries when the teams took to the ice that day. The Soviet Union had won the gold medal in five of the six previous Winter Olympic Games, which is why the US victory is widely regarded as one of the greatest upsets in the history of sports. All of the above made for a perfect Hollywood story, hence why Disney purchased the rights and created an exceptional movie.

What Disney could not have predicted was that the movie would provide unique insight into employment within a professional services world and become part of my Reflection Collection.

The particular scene that created this reflection revolves around the team's training camp when things aren't going quite right. Herb Brooks (the US Hockey team's head coach, played by Kurt Russell) is growing frustrated by the lack of unity within the team, and he is imploring them to be more selfless and work together. The US team was made up of collegiate hockey players that, while great individually, were used to playing for their respective universities and were now playing together for the first time. When Coach Brooks couldn't take their selfish play any longer, he provided them with an impassioned speech about teamwork and famously wrapped it up by telling them, "The name on the front of the jersey matters a hell of a lot more than the one on the back." It is a special scene and provided a glimpse into the growing teamwork that would become the trademark of this remarkable team.

This memory has stuck with me, but for a reason other than the standard American pride that grew out of the historic game. As it relates to athletic teams, I wholeheartedly agree with Coach Brooks's statement that the name on the front of the jersey matters more than the name on the back. Unfortunately, it has been my professional experience that too many sales and service professionals behave more like the 1980 hockey team before Coach Brooks's speech—and believe the name on the back of their jersey reigns supreme.

As with many things in life and business, you must find balance.

I spent my entire thirty-four-year career in the professional services arena selling, consulting, and servicing clients. During this time, I worked to build a personal brand of trust, integrity, and commitment. Given that I've never serviced or sold a widget, the name on the back of my jersey has been my currency, and my personal brand was developed by honoring my commitments, underpromising/overdelivering, and treating people with the respect they deserve. At Hewitt, we would often refer to this as building "trusted partnerships," and we were coached and mentored to ensure the commitments we made were genuine and the relationships we developed would be built on a foundation of trust.

Now, one could read the above paragraph and assume Hewitt was anti–Herb Brooks and they were creating an environment where everyone was in it for themselves and not focused on the broader team. Nothing could be further from the truth. You see, Hewitt recognized the name on the front of the jersey and the name on the back of the jersey are inextricably linked. One cannot survive without the other in a professional services world. Hewitt needed team members to recognize that the best salesperson, relationship manager, or consultant could not survive without a full team behind them rowing in the same direction and wearing the same jersey. *We* organizations > *me* organizations. Conversely, Hewitt would not have built the reputation it had within the industry without the personal brands of the individual salespeople, relationship managers, and consultants who were focused on building personal, genuine, and trusting relationships with their clients.

In today's world of sales and service, I too often encounter people who believe the name of the back of their jersey is far more important than the front and, similarly and equally unfortunate, organizations that believe the name on the front is more important than the back. In these situations, both sides are completely missing the point—the combined and coordinated strength of both names is required to produce a service that is capable of building trusted partnerships.

I have witnessed great salespeople move from organization to organization thinking their personal brand will carry the day and they can sell the proverbial ice to an Eskimo, regardless of the logo on the front of their jersey. However, the greatest ice salesman in the world will struggle mightily if there isn't a team behind them producing quality ice.

As you advance in your career, I encourage you to carefully consider the jersey you choose to wear and the logo that will be affixed to it. There must be strong alignment of your personal brand and the service culture of the organization. They are, most certainly, inextricably linked.

No one can dispute Coach Brooks is one of the greatest coaches (of any sport) of our time. However, if he had chosen to work within the professional services industry versus hockey, he would come to realize that the name on the front of the jersey is just as important as the name on the back.

CHAPTER 40

Lose Sight of the Shore

In any given moment we have two options: to step
forward into growth or to step back into safety.
—ABRAHAM MASLOW

A S NOTED PREVIOUSLY, my first Hewitt partner meeting in the fall of 1999 served as a watershed moment for my career. I had just achieved a significant milestone and could have chosen a simpler path from that point forward. However, instead of resting on my laurels, I opted to take the significant risk that came with joining Sageo, Hewitt's new healthcare business, ultimately resigning my partner status within one year of accepting it.

Given the first nine years of my Hewitt career were spent on the retirement side of the business, and I had only briefly dabbled in healthcare, joining a new business that was anchored on health insurance was a bit daunting. The CEO's request to have me join the new healthcare business was clearly based on the potential I brought to the table versus any specific healthcare knowledge I possessed. He must have been following Wayne Gretsky's recruiting analogy of hiring where the puck was headed, not where it was currently located.

As excited as I was to sit through the 1999 partner meeting and learn more about Sageo, I was equally as overwhelmed and a bit intimidated. I sat in the audience with divergent emotions—torn by the excitement to join this business and uneasiness of joining a business in which I was not entirely steeped. Waves of elation and inadequacy were continually washing over me. It would have been very easy for me to politely decline the CEO's invitation and swim back to the safety of my newly minted partnership shore.

Instead of allowing those thoughts to paralyze me, I opted to attack the opportunity. I bought books on e-commerce, read up on healthcare, and reached out to colleagues and mentors who were smarter than me on these topics—one of my original Wisdom Quests. I set up "Healthcare 201" sessions with my good friend Will Sneden for my daily commute home. Will was a healthcare actuary, Hewitt partner, one of my best friends at Hewitt, and soon-to-be fellow Sageo employee.

Will and I were roommates during my first year with Hewitt, and I considered him not only a friend but also a mentor. I would call Will on my drive home and pepper him with questions about healthcare—what were the challenges, what were the opportunities, and how could we solve them with Sageo? In times of uncertainty and feelings of inadequacy, I have found solace in turning to mentors for encouragement, guidance, and support. Will, along with a host of others, was critical in helping me gain comfort and confidence in this new arena. I was bound and determined to stretch myself and achieve success, but was smart enough to recognize my initial limitations.

My decision to be open to the opportunity, take the risk, and stretch myself turned out to be one of the best decisions ever made—not only for me but also for the Hewitt Orlando office. With my acceptance of the opportunity, Orlando became the epicenter for Sageo's operations—with both the technology and call center being staffed and led out of Orlando. This new business served as a catalyst for several years of growth in Orlando and created unique opportunities for a host of employees and leaders. My decision to take the risk and accept the challenge had a butterfly effect throughout Hewitt Orlando that continues today as the residual businesses that grew from Sageo in 1999 are still in operation.

I have pulled from this memory several times throughout my career and have freely shared it with others, as well. My oldest son, Sam, attended Georgia Tech and graduated with an industrial engineering degree. Upon graduation, he accepted a Memphis-based position with Smith & Nephew, a global medical device company. Following his first year, he was approached with an opportunity to temporarily relocate to Fort Worth, Texas, to work on a new project. Sam had just begun to set roots in Memphis and was really struggling with the decision. He questioned whether he wanted to inject such a challenge into an otherwise smooth sailing early part of his career. When he called me, I reflected on my decision to dive into Sageo and how the opportunity helped me grow, expand my knowledge and network, and learn from others. With that strong memory in mind, I encouraged him to jump at the opportunity, which he did. He stretched himself and took a risk to move to a part of the country where he knew no one, and it paid dividends for him.

William Faulkner famously wrote, "You cannot swim for new horizons until you have courage to lose sight of the shore."

My decision to swim for the Sageo horizon also gave me my first bite at the entrepreneurial apple, and I loved it. I identified that I love building businesses and trying out new things. Following Sageo's reintegration, I led Hewitt's foray into middle-market healthcare outsourcing, launched Hewitt's spending account business, joined Hewitt's emerging managed-BPO segment, and ultimately founded my own firm, MillsonJames. None of this would have been possible if I had listened to Tom Schmitz's (Sageo CEO) pitch, declined, and swam back to safety. Instead, my career trajectory was positively changed forever by having the courage to lose sight of the shore.

Since that 1999 leap of faith, my encouragement for others has always been to jump at new opportunities, take the risk, stretch yourself, and, most importantly, enjoy the journey.

CHAPTER 41

Trust the ROB Test

The only way to do great work is to love what you do.
—STEVE JOBS

I AM NOT ENTIRELY sure from whom I first learned of the roll-out-of-bed test (ROB test), but I have personally used it no fewer than a hundred times over my career, have witnessed it in action over a thousand times, and it has never failed. This lesson is a core belief for me, and I have shared it so freely because I firmly believe in its truth. The full axiom is as follows:

> If you do not *consistently* roll out of bed excited to go to work, it is time to find new work.

There are a host of variations of this principle (e.g., if you love what you do, you will never work a day in your life), and they all point back to the same thing—life is too short to not enjoy the work you perform Monday through Friday. As a leader, I often referred to this test when I spoke with a group of new hires or even during an interview process. I explained that "at [Hewitt Associates/PlanSource/MillsonJames/HUB], we want employees who are excited to be here, excited to serve our customers, and excited to work alongside people with similar goals and objectives. We want you to consistently roll out of bed in the morning excited to come to work, and if for some unfortunate reason, you lose that excitement, it is time for you to look elsewhere. Life is too short to live any other way."

One of the best examples of living out this principle for me was Joe Bialek, my manager at Hewitt in the late '90s. I joined Joe in opening the Hewitt Orlando office in 1997 and witnessed his daily passion for our associates and in serving our clients. It was clear to me Joe rolled out of bed each and every morning excited to go to work, consult with our clients, and lead our teams. His excitement and passion for Hewitt was real, and it was appealing. People wanted to be around that type of energy, and it allowed us to attract and retain some exceptional talent in the new Orlando market. Most everyone who worked with Joe found it easy to be tuned in to his frequency of excellence.

To help put this in perspective, when Hewitt opened the Orlando office, we had zero market credibility—no Central Florida resident knew who Hewitt Associates was. Given the size of the clients we were to initially serve, we needed to hire eighty-four people for our first hiring class. Attracting the right talent was going to be difficult, and we needed a leader who would personify Hewitt and would attract strong candidates—candidates who would excitedly roll out of bed every morning. Joe was the right man for the job. His passion created an attractive culture for Hewitt Orlando, which was an absolute must for us as we quickly grew from three to nearly two thousand employees within four short years. Even more impressive, of that initial class of eighty-four employees, there are several handfuls of them who still work for Hewitt/Alight twenty-seven years later.

Establishing and driving a company culture is an absolute imperative for a leader. Leaders must understand their customers will only love a company to the extent employees love their company first. Working backward from this, if employees do not wake up every day excited to come to work, then a customer will most certainly see right through this and walk down the road (or virtual road) to a competitor. Additionally, as a manager or leader, if you have identified a toxic person or personality who is causing disruption and is affecting the results of the ROB test for others, you may want to consider helping that person find the nearest exit.

Tony Hsieh, founder/CEO of Zappos.com, was someone with an unbridled passion for company culture and, although he didn't refer to it as this, ensured his employees consistently passed the ROB test. In his book *Delivering Happiness*, Tony shared how he made a bet with every new hire. His bet—after four weeks of training and a week on the job, all new hires were offered payment for their time plus a $2,000 bonus if they decided the company was not right for them and wanted to quit.[12] Said differently, if the new hire did not roll out of bed and get excited about the workday ahead, they should gracefully exit and find another company that could help them pass the ROB test. Amazingly, less than 1 percent of Zapponians took him up on his offer. While this approach is admittedly a bit extreme, those who knew anything about Tony (he tragically passed away in 2020), knew he was extraordinarily passionate about his company and would do anything to ensure his employees were living the Zappos culture on a daily basis, so much so that he put his money where his mouth was.

One of my favorite quotes from *Delivering Happiness* sums up why the ROB test is so important. Tony said, "I think when people say they dread going to work on a Monday morning, it's because they know they are leaving a piece of themselves at home."[13]

Don't allow any employee you lead to leave a piece of themselves at home. Train them. Encourage them. Challenge them. Listen to them. Reward them. However, if at the end of the day, they dread rolling out of bed to come to your office, then you should encourage them to find a place that will rid them of that dread.

The ROB test can be applied to all aspects of life, both professionally and personally. Life is simply too short to not love whatever it is you're doing, be it work, hobby, or a sport. I've witnessed the ROB test be applied in many personal situations, most recently with my youngest son, Caleb. Caleb is a natural athlete and played a host of different sports growing up. Midway through his middle school years, he began to narrow his athletic focus on the game of lacrosse, an exceptional sport and one for which he showed real promise and passion. He worked diligently on his craft and achieved great success, including making the varsity team as a freshman—a team that finished second in the state that year. However, his passion began to wane heading into his sophomore year and he didn't roll out of bed each morning excited to play lacrosse. Following his sophomore season, he applied the ROB Test and realized that he no longer had passion for the sport and shifted his attention and focus onto golf. He then poured his heart and soul into this new passion, loved it, and gained a skill that will serve him well as he moves forward in life and business.

As with anything, it is always good to understand where your passions lie. Find something that stirs your emotions and gets you excited to roll out of the bed in the morning. Life is too short otherwise.

One of the key elements of the ROB test is the word *consistently*. I can guarantee you will have a bad day with your current employer. It is bound to happen and you will most certainly struggle to find joy on a particular day. It may even be tough to roll out of bed the following day, or two or three. There is no such thing as a utopian employer—there will be good days and bad. What the ROB test is assessing is whether you *consistently* are energized to roll out of bed and get back to work. If you pass that test, you're in the right spot and you should work to maintain and replicate that feeling for you and your team. If you consistently fail the ROB test, it may be time for you to look elsewhere to consistently recapture the joy and energy you deserve.

A quote by Simon Sinek captures the ROB test perfectly. "Working hard for something we don't care about is called stress; working hard for something we love is called passion."

I am grateful for the passionate leaders with whom I worked over my career. These leaders not only established exceptional cultures but helped me understand the importance of doing so. They have each, collectively and individually, embodied the ROB test and helped me understand that, oftentimes, the most important people to an organization's culture are those who choose to leave.

CHAPTER 42

Freely Give What You Can Offer

The meaning of life is to find your gift.
The purpose of life is to give it away.
—PABLO PICASSO

RUNNING IS MY life's passion. I love all aspects of the sport—whether participating, spectating, or coaching. Additionally, running has served as a version of self-administered therapy for me. Whenever stress would befall me, I would go for a run, get my heart pumping, release the endorphins, and the stress would slowly start to melt away. If I had a difficult problem at work, I would lace up my running shoes, hit the pavement, clear my mind, and the solutions would suddenly become available. Some people find their best thinking comes in the shower—mine came to me around mile two of a solo run.

In addition to the therapeutic benefits, running also satisfied my competitive drive, as I competed in track and cross country for my high school and continued to run throughout college—particularly around exam time or when I needed to solve a particularly complex calculus problem. As an adult, my passion for running continued and I turned my attention to competing in marathons, completing a baker's dozen. Unfortunately, the excessive miles and my overactive genes caught up with me in 2007, when at the young age of forty, I was diagnosed with bilateral osteoarthritis in my hips and several doctors strongly recommended I find a new form of exercise. Even with that tough hand being dealt, my passion for the sport remained high and burns brightly even today, as I've been able to pour my passion into watching my wife and children run and compete in the sport I've loved most all my life.

My passion for running can be traced to a county-wide elementary school track and field meet that was held in my hometown of Orange Park, Florida. Each year, the eight or so elementary schools from Clay County would gather to compete in various track and field events, from the 100m to the 800m, including field events and relay races. We would compete against the fastest runners from each of the other elementary schools, with bragging rights and blue ribbons on the line. I absolutely loved it and it became one of my favorite days of the year. That meet was clearly the spark that lit the running flame inside of me that continues to burn today.

In the summer of 2005, I shared this memory with my wife and how appreciative I was for the people who hosted this track and field meet. Truth be told, I was actually complaining about how unfortunate it was that something like this didn't exist in our current hometown and how I wished our kids and their friends could have a similar opportunity. As any good spouse would do, Kristin turned the tables on me, gave me a swift kick in the shorts, and encouraged me to stop complaining and do something about it. That gentle "encouragement" hit me squarely between the eyes, and I quickly began calling local schools, running stores, and nonprofits trying to figure out a way to bring such an event to our community.

Slowly but surely, we picked up momentum, and six months later, hosted the first ever Fast Start Track and Field Invitational for the nine elementary schools that fed into our local high school. The initial meet had over 750 children sign up to participate, which exceeded my wildest expectations. Eighteen years later, the Millson family along with the nonprofit organization I founded (Fast Start Management), continues to host the annual event with over 1,000 children signing up each year! Our hope is that of the thousands of children who have participated in our event since 2006, more than a few flames have been ignited and have led to a lifelong love of running, just as my childhood event did for me.

The lesson learned through this experience was twofold. The first was to never complain about something unless you have a solution in mind, and I have reflected on this lesson many times throughout my professional career. President Teddy Roosevelt once said, "Complaining about a problem without offering a solution is called whining" and when you think of it in those terms, no one wants to be labeled a whiner. My wife appropriately encouraged me to stop whining and do something about it—and we did.

The other lesson I learned came from a friend who graciously offered his services eighteen years ago and continues to even today. His name is Ron Boucher, and I've often reflected on his response to a random email I sent his way in 2005. As I began researching how we could pull off an elementary school track meet of this magnitude, one of my first steps was to reach into the community to see if I could gather friends and colleagues to pitch in and help. I was looking for sponsors, contacts, introductions, and people who understood track-meet operations. Ron was one of the first people to respond, but he told me he had no contacts in track and field, he couldn't make any introductions, and had no insights into track meet operations. Instead, he reframed my question by telling me his God-given gift was branding, marketing, and graphic design and he would be more than willing to lend his expertise to support the cause.

Ron's willingness to offer something I hadn't even begun to think about is the key lesson I learned from this experience. Rather than ignoring my email or responding that he couldn't fulfill any of my stated requests, he freely gave what he could offer—his branding support. The way my brain operates, I wouldn't have come around to thinking about a logo or brand until much later. Even when I got around to thinking about it, I likely would have created something dreadful. Thankfully, he stopped me from perusing the (not so) wonderful world of clip art.

Being tuned in to Ron's frequency and appreciating his willing nature to share his excellence is what has stuck with me over the years and it has encouraged me to do the same ever since.

Too often, when someone asks for assistance, our minds immediately go to fulfilling the request as stated. Someone asks for A, B, or C, and we think whether we can deliver A, B, or C. The beauty of this lesson and the encouragement for each of us is that we should take a beat, zoom out, and think beyond the stated request. What is behind the request? Is there another way to view the request or situation? Or, simply, what can I offer to help this person? Professionally, this approach can be helpful in sales and service because often a prospect or a client isn't entirely sure what they are asking and they can use your help to reframe the question. In these situations, when you're able to take a step back and offer a different perspective, you've delivered real value. Just as Ron did with me in 2005.

Ron's support of our event has been exceptional and helped us create something special for our community. The kids love having a fresh, new Fast Start logo each year and proudly wear their Fast Start T-shirts throughout the year. That is, until they return 365 days later to compete, pick up a newly Ron Boucher-branded T-shirt, and (hopefully) further ignite their running passion.

I can't imagine their excitement would have reached the same level if I had taken that dreadful stroll through the clip art library back in 2005!

As Picasso noted so many years ago, "the meaning of life is to find your gift. The purpose of life is to give it away."

As a postscript to this chapter, it should be noted that Ron's willingness to freely give what he can offer continues, as he generously offered his creative expertise to help me develop this book's title, subtitle, and, most notably and appreciatively, the exceptional artwork that adorns the cover.

CHAPTER 43

Always Run to Something, Not Away

Don't be pushed around by the fears in your
mind. Be led by the dreams in your heart.
—ROY T. BENNETT

THROUGHOUT MY CAREER, I was unabashed to reach for
my mentors. It didn't matter the content or context, I would
reach for them whenever I was faced with opportunities, challenges, or difficult decisions. Sometimes I needed their advice; other
times, I needed them to challenge my thinking. Regardless of the reason, because our relationships had depth and were equally yoked, the
calls were always received and returned with appreciation and love.

Mentors are an invaluable resource. They share a personal connection with us and hold a unique understanding of our goals and
desires. The best mentors also have the ability to speak truth and
hold us accountable, even when the advice isn't exactly what we want
to hear—which was the case for me in learning this lesson.

During the second half of the 2000s, I was faced with a series
of self-inflicted career challenges as I considered leaving Hewitt
Associates and then, upon my exit, spent the ensuing four years
wondering if I had made a mistake. During this window, I was leaning
on two mentors in particular—my father (until his passing in early
2009) and John Bausch.

John, a former partner of mine at Hewitt, served as our chief customer experience officer at Sageo. As we launched the Sageo business, John and I spent a significant amount of time together. Through this challenging experience, we developed a very special relationship, and I came to deeply respect him for his brilliant mind and straightforward honesty. Combined, these qualities are incredibly powerful, and we should all aspire to have mentors with such abilities.

As I was contemplating a change in employment in 2009, I reached for John to get his perspective on the various options I was considering. The coaching John provided was not only helpful in that moment, but it quickly became part of my Reflection Collection in helping coach others.

As I spoke with John, I dumped all of my frustrations and misgivings upon him. He took the time to listen, allowed me to vent, and when I came up for air, he paused and asked me a critical question: "Are you running from something or are you running to something?" John will be the first to acknowledge that his question wasn't novel, but it was clearly the first time someone had presented it to me, and I was grateful, if not a little surprised.

He accurately observed that most of our conversation that day centered on the negatives of my current situation rather than the positives of my anticipated outcome. Additionally, he pointed out that better results are achieved when change is driven by clear excitement for the future rather than a desire to avoid present unhappiness. As was often the case with John's wise counsel, he was spot on—he helped me realize I was running away from something rather than toward something and it helped change my perspective.

To be clear, a bad situation isn't going to improve magically on its own. There are toxic or abusive situations that clearly require you to run away from something for your mental well-being. Fortunately for me, this was not my situation in 2009.

The key lesson I took from John's question was to recognize the importance of setting aspirational goals to drive actions. I needed to focus my energies on identifying the right, long-term next step for my career, which would naturally create a level of excitement to propel my future actions.

John's straightforward yet powerful question prompted significant reflection and challenged me to reframe my thinking, which it did. As a result, MillsonJames was successfully launched nine months later.

I have also applied this thinking to recruiting. During an interview, I ask probing questions to determine whether a candidate's passion is greater for joining us or leaving someone else. If it's the former, great. If it's the latter, thanks, but no thanks. You might be surprised at how easy it is to make this assessment. Start by asking why they are interested in joining ABC Company. If they spend more time discussing their current issues with XYZ Company than their excitement for joining ABC, you'll save yourself future hassle by moving on from that candidate.

This assessment should also be applied when coaching others. If someone approaches you about a potential transition, help them determine whether they are more passionate about the future or simply potentially relieved of their past. There's an old adage, "Your day will go the way the corners of your mouth turn." Ask them why they are looking for something new. If their response makes them frown as they discuss their current challenges, coach them to find a way to turn their corners upward and focus on excitement for the future. This might mean coaching someone to leave your organization, but if you care about the person or the company, you'll set aside that fear and freely pose John's question.

If you ever find yourself at a career crossroad, I would highly encourage you to reach for your mentors and ask them to help you make this assessment. Gaining an outside perspective from someone you care for and trust will almost always lead to a better outcome.

John Bausch served in this capacity for me in 2009, and I'm certain your chosen mentor can do the same.

It is always better to be excited for the future than to be relieved of the past.

CHAPTER 44

View Your Career as a Hockey Stick

Patience is necessary, and one cannot reap
immediately where one has sown.
—SØREN KIERKEGAARD

U PON GRADUATION FROM the University of Florida, I was ready to conquer the world. I was confident in my abilities and was excited to bring my energy, passion, and strong work ethic to Hewitt Associates every day. I was standing on the bottom rung of the corporate ladder ready to race upward at a breakneck speed.

Those first several years with Hewitt in Atlanta were foundational for me in many ways. I learned a great deal, was surrounded by exceptional leaders, and my responsibilities were progressing nicely. We moved from Atlanta to New Jersey in 1993 so that Kristin could pursue her doctorate in early childhood education, and I was fortunate to be able to stay with Hewitt and transfer to the New Jersey office.

I was quite pleased with my growth and development—until about my sixth year. I remember feeling anxious and looking to jump into new areas to advance my career. I felt I was ready to take quantum leaps forward but found myself stuck in the mud. Work was becoming a bit of a chore and my energy started to wane. I was pretty sure I knew what I needed to snap out of it—advancement or bust—whether that meant with Hewitt or with another organization.

As it turned out, what I really needed was a mentor to step in, gently smack me upside the head, and encourage me to seek out what I really needed—patience.

At the time, I was reporting to a Hewitt partner named Charlie Hanlon. Charlie was the quintessential Hewitt Associate—smart, hard-working, ambitious, and nice (SWAN was the acronym Hewitt used to describe these types of people). He was also a great leader of our office. Charlie and I happened to be working late one evening around the time that I was self-sabotaging with those thoughts of advancement or bust. He poked his head into my office to ask how I was doing, likely a very simple and rhetorical question. However innocuous the question may have been, it opened the floodgates.

I shared my frustrations and desire to move on to bigger and better things. I complained, "I'm still performing tasks similar to those I did while in Atlanta and am ready for new challenges and advancement." Charlie simply smiled and told me that he, too, was still performing tasks he had mastered many moons ago. He then shared how his perspective on those tasks had changed over the years—that those tasks were table stakes in our business and necessary building blocks for the future. He encouraged me to have patience, to keep my eyes focused on the road ahead and to not to lose sight or heart by looking too far into the future. My time would come, he encouraged me. Charlie also took the opportunity to gently remind me I still had areas to develop and experiences to gain in my current position—and he was right.

I remember that evening conversation like it was yesterday, and as a reflective leader, I have called upon this memory and shared Charlie's wisdom countless times over the years because of its insight and impact. It was a career-changing conversation for me as I took his counsel to heart, sat tight, sought out new opportunities to further develop my skills, and was invited into the Hewitt Partnership three years later.

Fast-forward twenty-plus years from that fateful evening, and I was introduced to another way to view the same coaching around patience, this time using a hockey stick as a metaphor.

Chris Gardner, CEO of HUB Florida, would counsel an employee to view their career along a hockey-stick-like growth curve. The early part of a career is to be spent on the low slope of the blade—growth, opportunity, and advancement are available, but it may come slower than initially anticipated. Along that low slope, discomfort and anxiety will most certainly build within a younger employee. They may feel they aren't developing, that they continue to perform tasks they believe they have already mastered, or they feel stagnant. In these situations, we, as leaders, must encourage the employee to be patient and to resist the temptation to pull the ripcord and exit because, if they do prematurely exit, they may be setting themselves up for unforeseen challenges downstream. Among those challenges are an elongated stay on the blade of the hockey stick and establishing a pattern of job-hopping that can be difficult to overcome once started.

Now, to be perfectly clear, I am not encouraging anyone to stick with a bad job, a bad boss, or a toxic culture. No one should ever work for a jerk. Instead, my encouragement is that if you find yourself on the low slope of the hockey stick blade, you should challenge yourself to understand the root cause of your discomfort or anxiety and ask, "Is it externally or internally driven?" If external (e.g., toxic environment), prepare to pull the ripcord. If internal, you should invest the time on the low slope of the blade, allow the foundation to be fully set, seek out unique experiences within your current situation, and know that the inflection point, the point at which the hockey stick extends upward at a forty-five-degree angle, is coming in due time.

One of my father's best friends from Harvard MBA School was a gentleman named Bill White. Bill and his wife, Jane, became fast and lifelong friends of my parents. Bill had an exceptional career of being chairman and CEO of publicly traded Bell & Howell and currently serves as a professor of engineering and science at Northwestern University. He also published an exceptional book in 2006 called *From Day One.* Within this book, Bill describes the same need for patience and encourages people to understand, "It is good to have ambition, just don't be driven by it. Before you try to push your way vertically to the next level, consider what you can accomplish by expanding horizontally."[14] Sage advice from someone who knows a thing or two about successful careers and leadership.

Had I allowed my frustrations in 1996 to reach a boiling point, if Charlie hadn't been working late that fateful evening, or if I hadn't been tuned in to the right frequency during his office visit, my career might have taken a very different path. If I had pulled the ripcord and tried to artificially shorten the low slope of the blade, my inflection point would likely have been pushed further out, and I may not have achieved my career objective of making partner.

Charlie's coaching served me well in 1996, and I have borrowed it liberally over the years to encourage others to be patient as they climb those first few rungs of the corporate ladder.

Expand horizontally first, then grow vertically.

Be patient.

CHAPTER 45

Find Your Sweet Spot

Find out what you like doing best and get
someone to pay you for doing it.
—KATHARINE WHITEHORN

I WAS A HIGHLY average baseball player growing up—never the worst player on my team, but certainly no one could argue I was the best. I had good speed on the basepath but tapped out once the Little League pitching mounds were pushed back in the move from Major to Senior Leagues. I could hit a fifty-mile-per-hour "fastball" traveling forty-six feet, but found it significantly more challenging to hit a curveball traveling sixty feet, six inches. It was at that moment I decided I would take my talents from running ninety-degree base-paths to running a 400m oval track (440 yards in my day).

Even though my baseball career was shortened because of a true lack of ability, I can still vividly recall the feeling when my bat connected with a baseball. I mean really connected. The swing felt effortless and yet it created an amazing result. This unparalleled sense of baseball joy occurs when a baseball connects with a bat in precisely the right spot—the sweet spot. Hitting a ball with the sweet spot of a bat doesn't happen every time, but once you've experienced it, you seek to replicate it every time you step to the plate.

I was first made aware that our professional careers also have a sweet spot during a 1997 training course offered by Hewitt Associates. It was in this training class that I was introduced to the term *career best* and that it could produce the same unparalleled sense of joy that I felt on the baseball field—when an effortless swing produced an amazing result. Since that time, I have been focused on creating career-best opportunities for myself as well as those I have led, mentored, or managed.

The opportunity to create a professional career best comes when you take the time to look both inward and outward to truly understand yourself and the markets that surround you. There are three key factors to self-identify when looking to create these career-best opportunities—talent, passion, and market opportunity (a.k.a. market demand). When you can create, fulfill, or even stumble into a role that finds the intersection of your talent, your passion, and fulfills a market opportunity you are likely to experience that same feeling for which every baseball player yearns—you will have hit the sweet spot and the role you are fulfilling will feel effortless, and you'll create amazing results.

I was fortunate to experience several career-best moments and each one came from being aware of and seeking to find that elusive sweet spot within a Venn diagram. There was one particular career-best moment that stands out for me—when I founded MillsonJames in 2010.

In the years leading up to 2010, I had been contemplating launching my own consulting firm and had been playing with several different business models in my head. As part of my MillsonJames Wisdom Quests, I set up a lunch meeting with one of my colleagues and good friends, Stephen Bruner. Stephen and I had worked together at CoAdvantage/PlanSource. He was a quintessential entrepreneur and was someone for whom I had the utmost respect. A year following my MillsonJames launch, Stephen went on to cofound the drinkware company, Corkcicle, and currently serves as their co-CEO.

Although Stephen had never worked a day at Hewitt Associates and wasn't familiar with the career-best training or vernacular, he and I talked about trying to create a business that would maximize my talents in managing client relationships, my passions in helping clients solve problems, as well as satisfying a market demand/opportunity in the realm of HR and benefits technology. It was during our lunch at Johnson's Diner in downtown Orlando that the business model for MillsonJames began to take shape, and it was launched within the year.

I firmly believe everyone has the opportunity to create career-best moments for themselves, but it requires a good bit of introspection, and it doesn't hurt to have friends and mentors help you independently assess your talents, passions, and market opportunities.

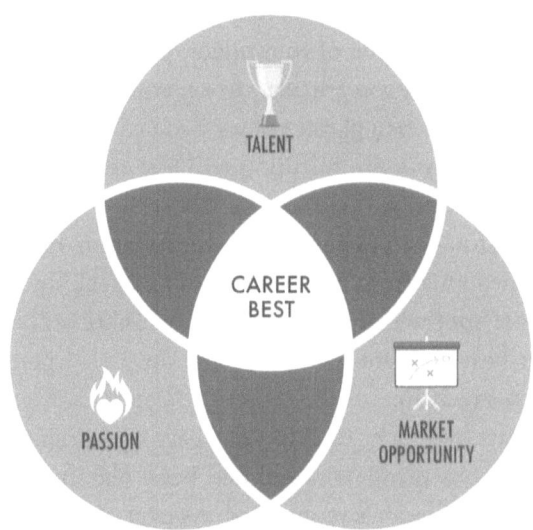

1. The first step is to identify your specific talent—What are you truly exceptional at doing? At first, your mind may drift to what you *enjoy* doing. While understanding what brings you joy is helpful (and will be addressed next), you need to look deeper into the skills you possess that separate you from the pack. What work do you perform better than the vast majority of those in your industry? It might be analyzing data, managing client relationships, networking, engineering

a solution, building an argument, or overcoming objections—whatever it is, identify it and work to create opportunities that allow you to demonstrate that talent on a daily basis.

Warning: If you are the absolute best at something in your industry, but lack the passion or there is no market opportunity, it is unlikely you'll achieve a career best. For example, if I happen to have a unique talent in singing (which I do not), but I lack the passion to perform or produce, then I will be challenged to find a career best in the music industry.

2.   The next step is to recognize your passion—what is it that pops you out of bed in the morning? What is that "thing" you do that brings a smile to your face and plays on a constant loop in your brain? What work do you perform that is effortless for you? What brings you joy or satisfaction? Here is one method I've used over the years to help someone identify their passions. I ask the employee to analyze their daily or weekly To Do List for a period of time. Whichever items seem to never get accomplished and keep rolling over from week to week, it is safe to assume they possess very limited passion for those items.

However, and conversely, the items that get checked off the list quickly and consistently, it is equally clear that those are the items about which they have a good degree of passion. For me, I always lean toward solving a client's problem—I will subordinate all other tasks to attack a client issue. For you, it might be helping others grow within their career, designing a new system/process, training, or managing a project to completion. Identifying your passion is critical, and it can take you very far in your career.

Warning: Passion without talent or an identified market opportunity will fall short of accomplishing a career best. For instance, I may have passion regarding architecture and truly appreciate how someone uses form and space to create something unique, but if I lack the talent and vision to do the same, there would (clearly) be no market demand for my drawings. As a result, a career best is highly unlikely for me in and around architecture.

3. The final step in trying to create a career best is to assess whether there is an existing market opportunity (or whether you could create a market opportunity). In this part of the introspection, what you're trying to assess is whether there is a customer base that will place value on the intersection of your talent and passion. For MillsonJames, my assessment was focused on whether I felt clients would find value and would be willing to pay for our consulting services around HR and benefits technology. Fortunately, there was market demand/opportunity for our services, which allowed me to achieve a career best and, once again, feel that sweet spot.

When my oldest son, Sam, was contemplating leaving his job with a Fortune 500 company and founding his own consulting firm, we sat down to identify his career-best opportunity. Much like Stephen Bruner did with me, Sam and I dissected his talents, passion, and market opportunity and identified that he, too, could create a career-best business by founding the Millson Group.** Sam launched his firm in 2020 and has been hitting the sweet spot in his career ever since.

While reading one of my all-time favorite books, *Atomic Habits* by James Clear, I came across a story that offered insight into how Scott Adams, the creator of the very funny comic strip *Dilbert*, used a variation of career-best thinking to produce an all-time great cartoon. Scott Adams said, "Everyone has at least a few areas in which they could be in the top 25 percent with some effort. In my case, I can

---

** It should be noted that we Millsons are not very creative when it comes to branding our companies—MillsonJames, The Millson Group, and my father's retail corporate name was Millson Enterprises. Suffice to say, the Millson family's career-best opportunities were not in and around marketing or branding.

draw better than most people, but I'm hardly an artist. And I'm not funnier than the average standup comedian who never makes it big, but I'm funnier than most people. The magic is that few people can draw well and write jokes. It's the combination of the two that makes what I do so rare. And when you add in my business background, suddenly I had a topic that few cartoonist could hope to understand without living it."[15] Scott Adams clearly found his sweet spot, and it produced amazing results (and a few million laughs).

I have been fortunate to have found the sweet spot of talent, passion, and market opportunities several times over my career and during those times, the work has been effortless and produced amazing results. I encourage you to involve others in helping you produce your own Venn diagram to identify your sweet spots and then work to increase the likelihood of finding those career-best moments.

I'm grateful for friends, mentors, and my ability to be tuned in to the right frequency during that 1997 training class to help me identify my career-best opportunities—because it was clear at an early age that no one, and I mean no one, was going to pay a dime to watch me try to hit a curveball.

CHAPTER 46

Always Take the Meeting

Don't judge each day by the harvest you
reap, but by the seeds that you plant.
—ROBERT LOUIS STEVENSON

A LLOW ME TO paint an all-too-common picture for you.
You receive an email, phone call, or social media message
asking you to meet or have a phone call with someone you
only casually know. Given that you anticipate they will be making a
pitch of some sort, you engage in serious mental gymnastics trying
to find a way to politely decline or devise an excuse not to meet.

Sound familiar?

I've been in your shoes. I have performed those same mental
gymnastics and I have come up with more dodges and excuses than
I care to recall. However, that all changed for me following two un-
related events that were quickly added to my Reflection Collection.
Ever since, whenever I receive one of these unsolicited requests, I
hear my friend Mary Tomlinson's voice tell me to "always take the
meeting," I reflect on a 2009 career-altering visit to Kansas City, and
then I happily accept the request.

As part of my 2010 MillsonJames Wisdom Quest process, I was
interested to meet with a woman named Mary Tomlinson from our
church. Although I knew her husband, Bill, I did not have much of
a relationship with Mary and thought it might be a bit of a stretch
for her to accept my invitation. Thankfully, she didn't see it that way

and agreed to have lunch. Mary was a former leader within Disney and had successfully launched her own management consulting business several years prior.

As had been the case with every other Wisdom Quest that summer, Mary provided me with specific and much appreciated advice that I have reflected upon frequently.

At some point in our meeting, I shared a story of how I had recently received an odd request from a LinkedIn connection and wasn't sure whether I wanted to meet with the person. Mary politely laughed at the obvious irony and then shared with me her philosophy of "always take the meeting." Given that I'm slow, I missed the irony and responded with initial skepticism regarding her advice. I said, "I cannot imagine how inefficient and annoying it would be if I had accepted the varied requests from vendors, salespeople, and would-be acquaintances over the years." She countered by sharing with me countless examples of random meetings that turned into downstream blessings and how the long-term value was often not immediately obvious. At the end of our meeting, I tucked away her advice with a hope to live it out, but if I'm being honest, I remained skeptical.

One year later, I was confronted with a powerful memory that pushed my skepticism to the side of the road and helped me fully appreciate Mary's advice.

The event occurred during a business trip to Kansas City while I was working for PlanSource. I was in town to meet with a few insurance agencies and had mapped out my schedule for the few days I'd be in town. Before my visit, I had received an email from a Kansas City–based contact asking if we could connect while I was in the area. I was initially hesitant because I wasn't sure the meeting would bear fruit and, as a result, I had not yet responded. After an exhausting round of mental gymnastics, I ultimately agreed to meet, but scheduled the meeting for the tail end of my visit, giving myself an out if something else came up.

As it turned out, that meeting served as one of the single greatest time investments of my career.

The person with whom I met that day was Kevin Murphy, who worked for an insurance company called Assurant. Kevin and I immediately hit it off—finding common grounds of family, running, and BBQ. We eagerly explored ways to work together and he shared some of the unique things Assurant was doing within their MVP program—a tier-based rewards program for their top insurance agencies around the country. We ultimately moved our meeting to the original Arthur Bryant's, where we broke bread and burnt ends. It was a great meeting and I returned home appreciative of my time with Kevin and thankful I found the time to meet with him while in Kansas City. However, and unfortunate for any potential partnership, I left PlanSource within the year.

Fast-forward two years and I had all but forgotten about my meeting with Kevin because partnering with insurance companies wasn't part of my original MJ business plan. Luckily for me, Kevin had not forgotten about our time together. He reached out in 2011 to congratulate me for launching MillsonJames and asked if I was interested in helping Assurant with a consulting project. Thankfully, my business plan was written in pencil and I eagerly jumped at the chance to support him. That project was successful and he hired us for another, which also went well.

With those two test projects behind us, Kevin approached me to ask if MillsonJames would be interested in becoming a strategic partner within their MVP program—essentially being *the* primary technology consultant for their MVP agencies throughout the United States. Without blinking an eye, I emphatically said yes, and Assurant began introducing us to their MVP agencies around the country and provided me with speaking opportunities at their annual conference.

With Assurant's nationwide salesforce helping distribute our services, the MillsonJames sales pipeline was suddenly overflowing, and we never looked back. All of this was possible because I reluctantly said yes to what I initially believed would be an extraneous meeting in Kansas City.

I will never again be so happy to be so wrong.

From that day on, even when the benefits of a meeting weren't immediately clear, I said yes to accepting meeting requests. When you take the time to meet with someone, be fully present with them, and invest in them, you are planting seeds. The seeds may not bear immediate fruit, but oftentimes, those seeds have the potential to produce something special for both parties. You never know from where your next great opportunity will come, yet you dramatically increase the potential for those opportunities when you take the time to expand your network and strengthen relationships—even when they don't initially make sense.

It is also helpful for you to remember there will be times when you are on the other side of these requests—you are the one reaching out to connect with someone, hoping they respond affirmatively. Personally, I am grateful Mary and others in my network agreed to meet with me when I was launching MJ and searching for wisdom. I can't imagine my path had any or all of them refused my invitation because they were too busy or didn't see an immediate benefit. I constantly remind myself of the graciousness of these colleagues, their willingness to meet with me, invest in me, and mentor me— particularly when their own mental gymnastics may have initially told them otherwise.

And when you do take that random, out-of-the-blue meeting request, be sure to tune in to the excellence that may soon surround you—it may not be immediately obvious.

Always. Take. The. Meeting.

CHAPTER 47

Diversity of Experience Is Key

There are not more than five musical notes, yet the combinations
of these five give rise to more melodies than can ever be heard.
There are not more than five primary colors, yet in combination
they produce more hues than can ever been seen. There are not
more than five cardinal tastes, yet combinations of them yield
more flavors than can ever be tasted.

—SUN TZU

HAVE YOU EVER felt a pit in your stomach, sensing you've
forgotten something or that something is missing? It's that
sixth sense we all have when something is amiss. It's like
Kevin's mother in *Home Alone*—she knows something isn't quite
right, and it's not just that they left the garage door open, as her
husband dismissively suggests. Nope, turns out it was a bit more
than that, Peter McAllister.

Well, my sixth sense was operating at full throttle during my latter
years at Hewitt. I had encountered a lifetime of positive experiences,
and yet I felt as though something may be missing. Something wasn't
quite right, and I developed that familiar pit in my stomach. Luckily
for me, I didn't leave an eight-year-old home alone at Christmas, but
something was definitely missing.

Hewitt was well known for doing things certain ways—some
would even refer to it as "the Hewitt Way." We had particular methods
to service customers, monitor financials, write client correspondence,

and even dress for client meetings. I loved it all and ate it up. I was convinced the Hewitt Way was, hands down, the best way to run a business.

To that end, we had a training class called "Charm School," during which we were trained on how to interact with our customers including, but certainly not limited to, where to sit in a client meeting (interspersed), how to sign in at the front desk (illegibly so that a competitor can't see you've visited), what not to discuss with a client (religion or politics), where not to place your briefcase (on the client's conference table), and in which hand you should hold your briefcase (your left so that you can shake a client's hands with your right). To a large degree, I still believe Hewitt's way was better than most. However, as I rounded the corner following my sixteenth anniversary, I knew something was missing, and I became curious how other organizations and industries operated.

I yearned for something new and different.

In life, we can generally agree that diversity of most anything yields a better result, whether it is diversity of thinking, culture, race, gender, or, as was the case with me after nearly seventeen incredible years with Hewitt, experience. I was seeking new experiences as my curiosity was pushing me beyond what I knew of the Hewitt Way. I wanted to surround myself with new people who had different experiences to become a better leader, manager, consultant, and person. So, after some of the best years of my life, I decided to leave the comforts of Hewitt to gain these new and diverse experiences.

With nearly two decades of hindsight, I can now say that aside from my decision to join Hewitt in 1989, my decision to leave the same was one of the better decisions of my professional career. Upon departing, I was exposed to a new set of leaders, was handed my first real P&L to manage, learned the similarities and dissimilarities of small- versus large-market customer service, and was forced to overcome new obstacles. Candidly, it was an initial shock to my system and I felt as though I had stepped through the looking-glass into uncharted territory. Yet, in looking back at those years, the diversity of those experiences deepened my abilities as a leader and served as a foundation and spark for my entrepreneurial endeavors. Although I had thoughts of launching my own firm in 2006 when I was considering leaving Hewitt, I likely would have failed without the diversity of experiences I gained after leaving the friendly confines of Hewitt.

I should clarify that my encouragement here is not to job hop every few years to accumulate experiences nor is it to say working with a single employer throughout your career limits your opportunities. The former is ill-advised as you do not want your resume to resemble a NASCAR vehicle with logos strewn about. For the latter, there is significant value for someone who chooses this path if you are able to seek out diversity within your organization. For someone who does work at a single employer, I highly encourage you to step out, try new things, transfer to another division, move to another office location, or all of these. Do whatever you can within your situation to increase the diversity of your experiences, work under different leadership, or learn a new market segment. I can assure you that you will be glad you did, even if it comes with some initial challenges. As my father's Harvard classmate Bill White noted—you should look to expand horizontally.

The Hewitt Way was crucial in helping this young professional learn the importance of teamwork, client service, quality, humility, and granting benefit of the doubt. I couldn't have asked for a better foundation and yet it also allowed me the ability to embrace the diversity of experience I gained upon leaving.

As with anything in life, seeking out and embracing diversity is a key to life's success.

CHAPTER 48

Above All Else, Choose Family

Family is not an important thing. It's everything.
—MICHAEL J. FOX

I MAKE THE FOLLOWING statement without any form of judgment, with great sincerity, and with full appreciation for other addictions—but I am a recovering workaholic. I come by it honestly, as my father was a recovering workaholic as well. As highlighted in the early pages of this book, it is remarkable how unbelievably parallel our two careers were in the decisions and sacrifices we independently made. I'm extraordinarily proud of my father's decision to choose family above all else in 1974, and it gave me the confidence to do the same thirty-six years later.

My father was a grinder. He grew up in a US Army household, constantly moving across the country and into foreign lands, including graduating from Yokohama High, an American high school on an Army base in Japan. As with any child of military upbringing, he mastered the craft of adapting to his surroundings and working hard to get ahead. At any given point during his teenage years, he would be working three, four, even five jobs to make sufficient money to pay for his collegiate schooling, which he voluntarily chose to do.

He initially attended the University of Washington until he withdrew to follow a girl across the country. Upon arrival in Washington, DC, he enrolled and ultimately graduated from American University, with honors. Alas, the girl he chased was not my mother, but his move to DC did allow him to meet my mother, Mary Louise James, after he and his cross-country love decided to go their separate ways. As a side note, if anyone was wondering who the James was in MillsonJames— you were just introduced to her. My mother was the last James in her lineage, and the name MillsonJames was created to pay homage to her.

Following an otherwise unspectacular beginning to his collegiate career in Washington, he took an immense flyer when he decided to apply for admission to one of the top MBA programs in the country—Harvard Business School. My father was not your prototypical Ivy League candidate as he came from little money and no Ivy League pedigree of which to speak. His ability to get into and, even more shockingly, pay for Harvard is a true testament to his ability to outwork everyone around him.

Upon graduation from Harvard, he went to work for Arthur Andersen in their corporate-audit division. If you know anything about Arthur Andersen (pre-Enron), they were a hard-charging Big Eight accounting firm that offered partnership as their brass ring and expected hefty, billable hours from their associates. My father was equally as hard-charging and worked tirelessly to not only provide for his family, but to rise the corporate ladder and take a run at partnership. He ultimately chose to leave Andersen and moved into corporate finance and accounting, working for organizations such as Intercraft Industries and Story Chemical, continuing to work up the corporate ladder and always outworking his counterparts. His nose was constantly pressed to the grindstone.

Due to some circumstances inside and outside of his control, my father ultimately left his position at Story Chemical and was faced with a difficult and career-changing decision: continue working his way up the corporate ladder or jump off the ladder, take a leap of faith, choose family, and open his own business. He chose the latter over the ladder, and bought a retail business in Orange Park, Florida in the summer of 1974.

Given I was all of seven years old, my memory isn't overly clear on the details of his transition from corporate America to entrepreneurship. However, I do recall a dramatic shift in the visibility of my father upon our move to Florida. Whether pre- or post-1974, my father was present in our lives and a great man. However, his decision in '74 opened up a new world to our family. He coached my brothers and me in our chosen sports and he never missed one of our football, basketball, baseball, soccer, swimming, cross country, or other nonathletic events. Never. This was clearly one of his primary objectives in taking that leap of faith in 1974 when he, very intentionally, chose to put family above all else.

However, the ultimate gift he gave me was the model he set in the choice he made—family.

Fast-forward to January 1990 as I join Hewitt Associates as a twenty-two-year-old associate, with big dreams and equally sized goals. From day one, my goal was to outwork everyone. I knew I was never going to be the smartest person in the room, but I could guarantee I would be the hardest working one. The good, yet challenging news for me, was that Hewitt placed a value on hard work and would measure our monthly hours, both billable and total, as one measuring stick for partnership consideration. I used the word challenging above because it was for me. When you combine the value Hewitt placed on hours worked, my insatiable desire to outwork everyone, and the aforementioned workaholism gene, you get a combustible situation. Working sixty, seventy, or eighty hours a week at Hewitt was not unheard of, and I actually hit a hundred hours in one, forgettable week. I ran exceptionally hard for my clients and it didn't hurt to know the partners were taking note of extraordinary efforts.

My wife, Kristin, was always understanding of the hard work that was required at Hewitt, and she was, for the most part, supportive. In the early years, I would often attempt to arrive at the office extra early to try and balance time at work and time with my new wife. Additionally, work on the weekends was limited to one day versus two in an effort to try and maintain some semblance of balance. It was a struggle, but I loved my work, and Kristin understood my goals and desires to make partner.

I wish I could say I found more balance once we had children, but for some odd reason, the opposite would often occur as I would be presented with a new project opportunity just about the time one of our children was born. The most startling timing was with our daughter, Rose, as she was born in August 1999, and I jumped into Hewitt's e-business, Sageo, in September of the same year. For the first two years of her life, I spent Monday through Thursday in either San Francisco or Chicago, running hard, building the business, yet, unfortunately, missing a good bit of her early years.

As diligently as I worked to try and minimize the impact on my family, it was becoming more and more difficult to do so. Family time was inconsistent, family dinners were equally erratic, and weekends were uneven with me having to go to the office for extended periods of time. Even upon achieving partnership, the hours didn't subside.

As with most addictions, enough is never enough, and I would find new reasons to continue to work harder than I had the year before. I knew something had to give, and yet I was unable to make any changes on my own.

Ultimately, it took the strength of my wife and the love of my family to break me from the grind and addictive behavior.

I don't recall the exact date, but I do remember the specific conversation my wife had with me in the spring of 2002. At the time, we had three children (Sam, six; Jesse, four; and Rose, two) and we were working hard to maximize family time and create a solid foundation for them. However, Kristin had reached a boiling point, and she was ready to create a more solid foundation for our family.

She began her march toward balance and stability by addressing the seemingly lost American treasure—family dinner. She made it crystal clear to me that, going forward, dinner would be served and on the table at 6:00 p.m. sharp, and I was expected to be there—consistently.

Message heard.

I was working from the Orlando office at the time and was one of the senior leaders and partners in the office. There was an unwritten rule and unfortunate stigma that if you left the office before 6:00 p.m., you weren't pulling your weight on the team. Some people even called it the "walk of shame" if you were to depart "early." I didn't create the rule, but I certainly adhered to it and unknowingly held others to this unwritten standard. Kristin's 6:00 p.m. dinner decree, while incredibly appropriate and necessary, was going to cause me to break this rule.

There was no decision to make, but I did need to communicate openly with my team regarding my new schedule. I sat down with everyone to inform them I would be leaving every day between 5:00 and 5:30 p.m. to make it home by 6:00 p.m. for dinner. I further explained that if anyone had a problem with it, I'd be happy to speak with them.

This decision was a turning point in my career and in the history of my family. It is a decision and outcome that I treasure to this day. It wasn't about cutting my office hours by thirty to sixty minutes. It was a mental and cultural shift not only for me, but for those I led.

Interestingly, the world continued to spin the following day. And the day after that. And the day after that. At work, my mentality began to change, and I became a better leader by recognizing and appreciating the need for balance in people's lives. I had always talked about balance prior to Kristin's dinner decree, but I truly began to lean into it, and, equally as important, I began to model this for others. I wouldn't slink out from 5:00 to 5:30 p.m. either. I would loudly pack up my briefcase and say good night to everyone as I walked out of the building. I was happy and excited to eradicate the walk of shame.

It should be noted that I do not blame Hewitt Associates or its leaders in any way for creating an environment that fed into my workaholism. That was my issue and mine alone. Anything taken to an extreme is unhealthy, and I allowed it to become just that. It should also be noted that I continued to work diligently at Hewitt as well as at all my downstream employers. I simply began working smarter, not harder. I am wired for striving for excellence in anything

I do, and I wasn't willing to change that part of me. However, my decision to choose family above all else was at the root of many, if not all, of my future career decisions.

My encouragement for you is, whether you are afflicted with the same challenges I had or not, you should always choose family—100 percent of the time. It is overly trite, but worth stating here: No one on their deathbed will proclaim they wish they had spent more time at work. No one. Take advantage of the opportunities you have to be excellent at work and excellent at home.

If you are ever faced with a career decision to choose family or business, the answer must be crystal clear—choose family. As a leader at work, you will help model this family-first behavior, and your impact will stretch well beyond your own home. Furthermore, when and if the time comes to raise a family, as a leader at home, you will be modeling this behavior for the very children with whom you're choosing to spend more time.

Just as my father so graciously did for me.

APPENDIX: RECOMMENDED READING

THE BOOKS NOTED below have rested either on my bedside table or been kept within easy reach on my office bookshelf throughout my career. Their pages are tattered, and their margins are filled with copious notes and annotations. They are all part of my Reflection Collection and they are well-thumbed.

Each of these books has played a significant role in my career, and I share them with you in the hope that they can be equally impactful for you.

I am deeply grateful to each of the authors, and I hope you come to appreciate them as much as I have.

Atomic Habits, by James Clear
Delivering Happiness, by Tony Hseih
Execution, by Larry Bossidy and Ram Sharan
From Day One, by William J. White
From Strength to Strength, by Arthur C. Brooks
Good to Great, by Jim Collins
It's Your Ship, by Captain D. Michael Abrashoff
Raving Fans, by Ken Blanchard and Sheldon Bowles
Ruthless Trust, by Brennan Manning
Selling the Invisible, by Harry Beckwith
The Coffee Bean, by Jon Gordon and Damon West
The Elements of Style, by William Strunk, Jr. and E.B. White
The Energy Bus, by Jon Gordon
The Infinite Game, by Simon Sinek

The Leadership Secrets of Colin Powell, by Oren Harari
The Obstacle is the Way, by Ryan Holiday
The Wisdom of The Bullfrog, by Admiral William H. McRaven
Trusted Partners, by Jordan D. Lewis
Unreasonable Hospitality, by Will Guidara

ENDNOTES

1   Arien Mack and Irvin Rock, *Inattentional Blindness* (Cambridge: The MIT Press, 2000).

2   Christopher Chabris and Daniel Simons, *The Invisible Gorilla* (New York: Crown Publishing, 2009).

3   Olivet Nazarene University, https://www.olivet.edu/research-statistics-on-professional-mentors.

4   Marshall Goldsmith, https://marshallgoldsmith.com/articles/try-feedforward-instead-feedback/.

5   Will Guidara, *Unreasonable Hospitality* (Optimism Press, 2022), 192.

6   Vince Clortho, "Lessons on Customer Experience from a New York Restauranteur," *The CEO Magazine*, https://www.theceomagazine.com/business/management-leadership/will-guidara/.

7   Mayo Clinic, "Stress Relief from Laughter? It's No Joke," https://www.mayoclinic.org/healthy-lifestyle/stress-management/in-depth/stress-relief/art-20044456.

8   Jim Collins, *Good to Great* (New York: HarperCollins Publishers, 2001), 35.

9   Colin Powell, *It Worked for Me: In Life and Leadership* (New York: Harper Perennial, 2014; originally published 2012), 223.

10   Oren Harari, The Leadership Secrets of Colin Powell (New York: McGraw-Hill, 2002), 215.

11   Mike Abrashoff, *It's Your Ship*, (New York: Warner Books, 2002), 47.

12   Tony Hsieh, *Delivering Happiness*, (New York: Business Plus, 2010), 153.

13   Hsieh, 171.

14   William J. White, *From Day One*, (New Jersey, Pearson Education, Inc, 2006), 132–133.

15   James Clear, *Atomic Habits* (New York: Avery, 2018), 225.

ABOUT THE AUTHOR

Scott Millson is a (mostly) retired executive who has dedicated the second half of his career to helping people find their frequency of excellence and grow their careers. He has held many titles along the way, including Founder, President, Partner/Owner, Chief Operating Officer, and before all those, Petty Officer Second Class (US Navy). Scott has worked with and for world-class organizations and leaders. Now, as an author, keynote speaker, and dedicated encourager, he spends his days helping others tune in to the everyday—but not always obvious-—crucial lessons of life and leadership.

Scott and his wife Kristin live in Winter Park, Florida and enjoy life's greatest spectator sport—watching their four grown children (Sam, Jesse, Rose, and Caleb) live their lives and find their own frequency of excellence.

Scott is pleased to author this first book in hopes that it encourages you to find the excellence that surrounds you.

Tune in!